DOORWAYS TO DECEPTION

DOORWAYS TO DECEPTION

How Deception Comes,
How It Destroys
and How You Can Avoid It

by
Mac Hammond

Harrison House
Tulsa, Oklahoma

Doorways to Deception—
How Deception Comes, How It Destroys and How You Can Avoid It
ISBN 1-57794-240-X
Copyright © 1999 by Mac Hammond
P. O. Box 29469
Minneapolis, Minnesota 55429

Published by Harrison House, Inc.
P. O. Box 35035
Tulsa, Oklahoma 74153

Contents

Contents

"Oh, God. Here we go again!"

Bob and Susan—a warm, likable couple and faithful church members—had just received yet another piece of negative news. This time it was regarding the health of their youngest child. A few months earlier, Bob had lost his job and had been unable to find another with comparable pay. Before that, Susan had faced a terrifying health crisis of her own. And before that, there had been a fire.

"When will it end?" they asked. *"Has God abandoned us?"*

Fair questions.

As a pastor, few things grieve my heart more deeply than seeing spiritually hungry, committed believers—saints who have a glorious inheritance in the kingdom of God— experience one calamity after another.

For some, the full-blown effects of "the curse"—the tragic result of sin and the Fall pronounced in the Garden of Eden and itemized in Deuteronomy 28—just seem to follow them around.

Ultimately, such calamity draws many of these people away from the Body of Christ after years of faithfulness. Later I hear that the life they once knew in Christ is all but destroyed. Sadly, a few end up living as if they had never made Jesus their Lord at all—if you want to call existing without the peace, presence and power of God "living."

Of course, Bob and Susan's story and the stories of so many others like them beg the question, "How does this happen?"

We know the Bible declares, **The curse causeless shall not come** (Prov. 26:2). So what is the cause that allows the devastating effects of the curse to devour precious people of God?

As I sought to understand the reasons why, the Lord began to reveal some truths to me in His Word.

First, I began to see that there is very little the devil can do in believers' lives without first *deceiving* them in some area. Invariably, it is deception in some area that creates an opening for the devil to do his work: to kill, steal and destroy. (John 10:10.)

Second, I saw that there are *certain things we do* and *attitudes we hold* that tend to open our minds to Satan's lies and make us more susceptible to such deception by the devil. These are the "doorways" to deception.

But once you are aware of these doorways, you can close them! When you seal those entry points, Satan will have drastically less access into your life and very few avenues through which he can touch your life with the effects of the curse.

Sadly, most Christians never realize that deception is the root of their experiencing the curse of the Fall. The purpose of this book is to change that.

You see, I don't want you to squander a lifetime blaming Satan—or worse, blaming God—for every negative circumstance you experience, unaware of an area of deception that is actually the root of the trouble.

My mission is to help you avoid being deceived into making wrong choices that allow the effects of the curse into your life.

I praise God that He has given us an infallible standard of truth, His Word, that makes avoiding or even destroying such deception possible. I have written *Doorways to Deception* to point out the kinds of things the Bible says open us to being deceived and thus ultimately damaged by Satan.

As you read these pages and study the Scriptures I cite, I pray that the Spirit of Truth will reveal to you the tactics Satan uses against God's people, so that, forewarned, you may be able to escape all the traps of the enemy—or, as Paul told the Corinthians,

In order that no advantage be taken of us by Satan; for we are not ignorant of his schemes.
—2 CORINTHIANS 2:11 NAS

CHAPTER I

The Father of Lies

*The spirit I have seen may be the
devil: and the devil hath power to
assume a pleasing shape.*

—William Shakespeare

Inch by inch the enormous wooden horse creaked and groaned its way ever closer to the massive gates of the impregnable fortress city—Troy.

According to Greek legend, this "Trojan Horse" represented the last, desperate attempt by the forces of the Greek city-state Sparta to defeat Troy and thereby return the beautiful, captive Helen to her rightful husband—Sparta's king, Menelaus. Spartans presented the giant horse as a peace offering, but the belly of this beast harbored a force of elite Spartan warriors.

You know the rest of the story. Troy opened the gates to receive the "gift." But when night fell, the soldiers of Troy, so relieved that the long Greek siege of their city was over, let down their guard and threw a drunken party. That's when Spartan soldiers fell upon the city.

A simple deception accomplished what years of applied brute force could not. Troy believed a lie. And Troy fell.

Similarly, when Adam and Eve believed a lie, mankind fell.

Today, countless believers fall for the same reason. Every day children of God experience destruction in some area of their lives simply because they have been deceived. In fact, I want to show you that deception isn't just *one* of the ways the devil can bring the effects of the curse into your life—it is the *only* way. I want to take you on a journey through the Word of God and help you discover this wonderful, life-changing truth: *If Satan can't deceive you, he can't defeat you.*

It is a profoundly simple truth that tragically few Christians understand.

To truly grasp the significance of how limited the devil is in his ability to touch the believer and how important a weapon deception is in his arsenal, you must first understand the nature of Jesus' victory over him. Only then does your need to guard against deception come into sharp focus.

Satan's Defeat

The death and resurrection of Jesus Christ represents *the* decisive moment in history. One theologian called the Cross "the hinge upon which the whole door of human history swings."

When Jesus conquered death and walked out of that garden tomb, something fundamental changed about Satan's authority in the earth. Although the devil was not yet completely bound, he had been stripped of all legitimate authority and power.

This truth of the devil's defeat is at the heart of the stunning, behind-the-scenes glimpse of Jesus' victory that Paul gives us in Colossians 2:15:

And having spoiled principalities and powers, he [Jesus] made a shew of them openly, triumphing over them in it.

Many Christians fail to grasp the full implications of the word picture Paul paints here. You see, Paul was a Roman citizen. He was familiar with the Roman method of celebrating a victory in war.

When a victorious Roman general, such as Julius Caesar, returned from battle, he reentered Rome with a parade. He and all his troops marched through the streets of the city leading their prisoners—the conquered soldiers of the enemy army—in chains.

At the center of this processional walked the king of the defeated country—shackled, beaten, his head shaven, utterly humiliated and completely stripped of power.

Paul uses this same image to describe Jesus' victory over Satan and his armies of demons. You get a little clearer picture of this in some of the other translations of this passage:

When He had disarmed the rulers and authorities, He made a public display of them, having triumphed over them through Him (NAS).

And having disarmed the powers and authorities, he made a public spectacle of them, triumphing over them by the cross (NIV).

A public spectacle! Can you see it? Can you picture the victory parade throughout the courts of Heaven when Jesus made a public spectacle of Satan?

For at least 5,000 years Satan had enjoyed a legal right to exercise dominion on the earth. Why? Because God had delegated dominion over the earth to the first Adam, who in turn had surrendered it to the devil through his rebellion in the garden.

Now, the "last Adam"—God in the flesh, Jesus Christ—has legally stripped Satan of that authority and restored it to man, reducing Satan to the status of outlaw in the process.

Jesus predicted the ultimate defeat and "spoiling" of Satan when He explained to the Pharisees His ability to cast out demons:

> But if I cast out demons by the finger of God, then the kingdom of God has come upon you. When a strong man, fully armed guards his own homestead, his possessions are undisturbed; but when someone stronger than he attacks him and overpowers him, he takes away from him all his armor on which he had relied, and distributes his plunder.
>
> —LUKE 11:20-22 NAS

The spoils Jesus plundered were the countless souls of mankind, held captive to sin and death by the fall of Adam.

In the following passage, Paul again refers to Jesus' spoiling of the underworld:

> Therefore it says, "WHEN HE ASCENDED ON HIGH, HE LED CAPTIVE A HOST OF CAPTIVES, AND HE GAVE GIFTS TO MEN." (Now this expression, "He ascended," what does it mean except that He also had descended into the lower parts of the earth? He who descended

is Himself also He who ascended far above all the
heavens, that He might fill all things.)

—EPHESIANS 4:8-10 NASB

By exercising His authority over demons during His earthly
ministry and by definitively defeating Satan through His resurrection, Jesus forever altered the devil's rights and abilities—
particularly where born-again believers are concerned:

...through the resurrection of Jesus Christ, who is
at the right hand of God, having gone into heaven,
after angels and authorities and powers had been
subjected to Him.

—1 PETER 3:21,22 NAS

Since the day Jesus stripped him of all his legal author-
ity, the only weapon Satan has left to use against the child of
God is the one he had to begin with back in the Garden of
Eden—deception.

In other words, because Jesus restored dominion to
redeemed man, Satan can't make you sick, rob your finances,
destroy your marriage, steal your kids or ruin your life—at
least not without first deceiving you in some way.

Now, please don't take offense at what I am about to tell
you. But the simple truth is, if you are not getting victory
over the curse in your life, the root of the problem is deception in some area of your life.

Don't let that insult you. We all—myself included—
harbor hidden assumptions and beliefs that don't line up with
the truth of God's Word. And that is precisely what deception
is—believing something contrary to God's revealed truth. The

very process of growing as a Christian is a matter of being transformed by the renewing of our minds. (Rom. 12:2.)

Furthermore, by its very nature deception is something we are unaware of in our lives. Think about it. Once you discover you have been deceived about something, you are not deceived anymore!

The Father of Lies

Because we live in a sin-cursed world, we will experience contrary circumstances, symptoms of lack or sickness or negativity from time to time. But if you are not experiencing increasing freedom from the curse, then there must be an area of deception somewhere in your life. We know this is so because Jesus said if we abide in Him, we will know the truth and the truth will set us free. (John 8:31,32.)

So let's begin uncovering deception in our lives by looking at the truth we find in Deuteronomy 30:19:

I call heaven and earth to record this day against you, that I have set before you life and death, blessing and cursing: therefore choose life.

Here, God is plainly telling us that the choices between life and death and blessing and cursing belong to us. God doesn't make those choices for us!

Now, if the God who loves you will not override your right to choose or oppose blessings for your own good, then He certainly will not allow Satan to override that right and impose his will on you either.

Satan cannot afflict you with the destructive effects of the curse unless you allow it by choosing, with your own free will, something that opens you up to those effects.

Think about it for a moment. Satan is not called the father of destruction; he's called the father of lies. If Satan had the power to destroy you, he would have already done so. But he can't. As it says in Proverbs 18:21: **Death and life are in the power of the *tongue*.** The power is in your tongue!

And Hebrews 2:14 says,

That through death he [Jesus] might destroy him that had the power of death, that is, the devil.

Ephesians 6:11 confirms this truth:

Put on the whole armour of God, that ye may be able to stand against the wiles of the devil.

Notice this verse doesn't say you are standing against sickness or poverty or some other crisis. No, you are standing against **the wiles of the devil**. *Wiles,* as defined in my concordance, simply means "trickery."[1]

The armor spoken of in the verses that follow is not given to you to protect you from negative circumstances; it's designed to enable you to stand against the root cause of all of Satan's attacks, which as we have seen is *deception*.

We see this very same truth in Revelation 20:1-3:

And I saw an angel come down from heaven, having the key of the bottomless pit and a great chain in his hand. And he laid hold on the dragon, that old serpent, which is the Devil, and Satan, and bound him a thousand years, and cast him into the

**bottomless pit, and shut him up, and set a seal upon
him, that he should deceive the nations no more.**

Do you see it? The Word doesn't say that Satan will no
longer cause famines and sickness. It doesn't say that he will
no longer cause anger and hatred or wars and killings.
Rather, the root cause of those things will cease. He will
deceive no more.

It would be helpful at this point to define what it means
to deceive. To deceive someone is to convince him that
something is true or valid when it is actually untrue or
invalid. You see, no one intentionally chooses destruction or
the curse. No, the only way Satan can defeat people is by
getting them to believe something that is untrue and invalid.

In other words, Satan can't bring evil into your life unless
you, in effect, choose it. And you won't choose it unless he
can deceive you into believing a lie.

Remember, God says you will experience life on the basis
of the choices you make. That's why He exhorts us in
Deuteronomy, "Choose life!"

Knowing this, Satan labors to deceive you in order to get
you to make destructive choices.

Basically, deception occurs when you choose to believe
something that is untrue—which is anything contrary to
God's Word, the Bible. Thank God, His Word *is* truth, and
the truth sets you free!

But if you don't know the truth, you have no way to
identify deception. Deception is easy to spot when you know

the truth! Yet I see committed believers drawn off and led astray by it all the time.

How does this happen to believers, some of whom even spend years in the Word of God? Invariably, it happens because they open a door in their lives for the devil to deceive them. When they believe and act on the lie, they inadvertently choose destruction and the curse. And Satan can damage or destroy their lives as a result.

Make no mistake about it—Satan is a liar and a very good one. But the Bible says we are not to be ignorant of his devices. The Word shows us how Satan comes to deceive, thus enabling us to foresee evil and avoid it. We can choose life and avoid Satan's deceptions!

CHAPTER 2

Satan is neither omnipotent nor free to do everything he pleases. Prince of the world he may be but the Prince of Peace has come and dealt him a death blow.

Holes In Your Armor

—Harold Lindsell[1]

One is hard put to find anything positive to say about the devil. If there were any good to say about him, it might be that he doesn't have any new tricks up his sleeve. In fact, he is spectacularly lacking in imagination. (Of course, that should be expected because God is the Creator and, therefore, the sole possessor of creativity.)

Because the devil has not learned any new tricks, everything we need to know about how to stand against his schemes is already written down for us in the Word of God. It is all still valid. No "revised and expanded" edition is needed.

First Corinthians 10:13 brings us this good news on the subject:

> **There hath no temptation taken you but such as is common to man: but God is faithful, who will not suffer you to be tempted above that ye are able; but will with the temptation also make a way to escape, that ye may be able to bear it.**

In other words, the devil has no new tricks—and no old tricks that you can't overcome.

Still, every minute of every day countless believers fall for the same tired old traps. I am convinced that we are ignorant of his schemes because of ignorance of God's Word.

For instance, Ephesians 6 enumerates some of the most common doorways to deception. In the form of a list of "armor" we need to protect ourselves from attacks of the enemy, God's Word lays out the various areas in which we are vulnerable to deception. Let's take a look at the entire passage, and then we will examine each piece of armor for insights on common deceptions:

> **Put on the whole armour of God, that ye may be able to stand against the wiles of the devil. For we wrestle not against flesh and blood, but against principalities, against powers, against the rulers of the darkness of this world, against spiritual wickedness in high places.**
>
> **Wherefore take unto you the whole armour of God, that ye may be able to withstand in the evil day, and having done all, to stand. Stand therefore, having your loins girt about with truth, and having on the breastplate of righteousness; and your feet shod with the preparation of the gospel of peace; above all, taking the shield of faith, wherewith ye shall be able to quench all the fiery darts of the wicked. And take the helmet of salvation, and the sword of the Spirit, which is the word of God: praying always with all prayer and supplication in the Spirit, and watching thereunto with all perseverance and supplication for all saints.**
>
> —EPHESIANS 6:11-18

It is important to understand that Ephesians is a book addressed to *believers*. It's telling believers how not to be deceived. You see, people who don't know Jesus as their Lord and Savior are already living in deception. The Bible tells us, **The god of this world** [Satan] **has blinded the minds of the unbelieving** (2 Cor. 4:4 NAS).

Theirs is the worst deception of all—the failure to recognize their need for Jesus. But as verse Ephesians 6:11 tells us, even Christians, who can be free from deception, are far from being immune to it:

> **Put on the whole armour of God, that ye may be able to stand against the wiles** [or deceptive strategies] **of the devil.**

This makes it clear. The role of this armor is to keep you from being deceived by the devil, and each piece symbolizes an area of your life by which Satan tries to deceive.

Notice that we are instructed to put on our armor.

In other words, God won't put it on for us. Each of us is responsible for putting it on ourselves.

Now, before we examine each individual piece of armor, let's look at the primary forms of deception we must guard against.

The Deception That the Devil Is Not Real

We see Satan's first and most basic deception in Ephesians 6:12:

> **For we wrestle not against flesh and blood, but against principalities, against powers, against the rulers**

of the darkness of this world, against spiritual wickedness in high places.

Satan is not a metaphor. He is not a symbol. He is not an
ancient and outdated method of explaining the human
propensity for evil. He is a real personal entity. And his first
attempt at deception will be to convince you that he isn't.

It is amazing how successful he is—even among suppos-
edly Bible-believing Christians. As recently as 1994, 59 percent
of Americans surveyed indicated a belief that Satan is not a
living being but merely a symbol of evil.[2]

It is easy to understand why this would be the first and
primary deception. If the devil can get you to believe that he
doesn't exist, you won't bother guarding yourself against
any of his other deceptions.

The devil doesn't want you to realize that he sponsors
the evil in your life. But you must understand that Satan is a
very real enemy who is very interested in your destruction.
You need to respect—but not fear—his ability to deceive you,
which will lead you down the road to death. As Jesus said:

> The thief cometh not, but for to steal, and to kill,
> and to destroy: I am come that they might have life,
> and that they might have it more abundantly.
>
> —JOHN 10:10

And there is a flip side to this coin of deception. The
devil knows that if he can keep you from seeing *him* as the
real enemy in your life, then you will see the people around
you as the enemy. You will be deceived into thinking that
you wrestle against flesh and blood.

Your problem is not your spouse, your boss, your family or any natural thing, because the battle is not fought in this natural world. As Ephesians 6:12 says, you wrestle against principalities, powers, rulers of darkness and spiritual wickedness. At the head of that realm of darkness is Satan.

The Deception That You Can't Win

If his primary attempt at deception fails, Satan has a plan B.

Once you acknowledge that Satan really exists and that he—not people or circumstances—is your true adversary, he will try to push you into the ditch on the other side of the road by selling you the lie that you are helpless to resist his attacks. He will try to convince you that you are powerless to keep him from bringing death and destruction into your life.

Of course, this is a lie. Remember, verse 11 instructed you to put on the whole armor of God *that ye may be able to stand* against the wiles of the devil. It *is* possible to stand successfully against anything the enemy can throw at you. So who can the devil overcome? We get some insight into that question in 1 Peter 5:8, which says,

> **Be sober [sound minded], be vigilant; because your adversary the devil, as a roaring lion, walketh about, seeking whom he may devour.**

The devil can't devour just anyone. His roar is designed to help him identify whom he *may* devour.

Satan will roar at you through false symptoms of sickness and disease. He will roar at you with fearful thoughts of financial difficulty. He will roar at you through marriage and family troubles. He will roar at you with thoughts that you will never do anything good for God.

Why does Satan come to you as a roaring lion? He does so for the same reason an actual lion roars at its prey: He wants to paralyze you with fear. You see, fear will produce either paralysis or panic. One stops you cold in your tracks and keeps you from resisting him. The other will cause you to quickly make destructive choices. Either way, if you succumb to fear, you allow the devil to devour you.

I am troubled at the number of believers I see held in the grip of fear. I believe no other single factor has more impact on our success or failure than our ability to handle the force of fear. Fear is a deadly thing—and it is much more powerful than people realize.

Think about it. From our earliest childhood, Satan begins subtly programming us to live in fear. He introduces fear into our relationships. He hounds us with fears of being rejected, scorned or abandoned.

Fear also affects our attitudes toward material possessions. For example, take a look at the way we handle our money. All too often, fear shapes the way we invest it, the way we spend it and the way we treat other people who might need some of it. The fear of poverty is a powerful stronghold in many a Christian's life.

There is no doubt about it: Fear is a prevalent, powerful and deadly force. Why is it so lethal? Because at a spiritual level, fear is a perversion of faith! To fear is actually to have faith in negative circumstances rather than faith in God's

Word. In other words, you have more faith in the devil's power to harm you than in God's promise to protect you.

Just as surely as faith moves the hand of God, so fear opens the door to the devil. That's why, as a Christian, you cannot afford to be complacent about fear. You must identify it and conquer it.

Of course, not all of the fear that invades your heart and mind announces itself by producing intense anxiety or a pounding pulse. Sometimes fear is stealthy—like our Air Force's stealth bombers. And in more mature believers, fear will often try to fly in underneath their "spiritual radars." You see, fear is more than an emotion; it is a spirit.

How then can you identify fear when it is trying to operate in your life? You can look for one of two things: panic, which can also appear as rage, or paralysis. One or the other of these conditions is an indicator that fear is working in you. Let me explain.

The first effect—panic—is by far the most visible and blatant manifestation of the force of fear. Panic produces an irrational and often irresistible desire to run away.

At other times fear expresses itself in the form of rage. When panic sets in, we may lash out at someone who is not really part of our problem at all.

Psychologists have a name for these two reactions. They call it the "fight or flight" response. These reactions are the most easily recognized manifestations of fear, but they are *not* the most dangerous.

No, the most damaging effect of the force of fear is paralysis. And it is far more dangerous because it is so subtle.

On many occasions I have seen the force of fear "freeze" people into staying in destructive situations. This is the so-called deer-in-the-headlights effect. A deer crossing a highway will see the lights of an oncoming car and simply freeze. The outcome is usually not pretty.

This type of paralysis is often fear's most damaging effect because it achieves the devil's goal of keeping you from doing *anything*.

Satan wants to neutralize your God-given power to change your life by trapping you in indecision. Let me illustrate what I mean.

A while back I spoke with a woman who was having tremendous difficulty quitting smoking. She knew she *ought* to quit. In her heart, she genuinely *wanted* to quit. But she couldn't. Why?

As I questioned her further, I discovered that she feared gaining weight once she stopped smoking. Every time she began to muster the resolve to quit, that spirit of fear crept in and whispered: *You're going to get fat. No one will like you. Your husband will probably leave you....* And so on.

The result was a deadly paralysis through indecision.

Think about that for a moment. This woman was risking cancer, heart disease and emphysema (not to mention compromising her Christian witness) because a subtle, secret fear produced paralysis in her life.

But don't think for a moment that women are the only ones subject to fear-induced paralysis.

A man came into my office some time ago who had been praying and believing for a new and better-paying job. He had worked at his present job for ten years and had advanced as far as he could. He was totally dissatisfied, unchallenged and unfulfilled. What's more, his family was struggling financially.

Then he heard me teach some of the principles of faith and decided, *Hey, I am going to use my faith and pray for a new job!*

Not surprisingly, it wasn't long before he was offered a new job opportunity. That is what brought him into my office that day. Instead of rejoicing that his faith had worked, he was standing there fretting!

"I've been thinking," he said. "What if I take this job and it doesn't work out? I mean, there is no guarantee that I will like this job any better. In fact, I could be worse off than I am now!"

What do you think he did? You guessed it—nothing. He stayed right where he was, paralyzed by the force of fear. And he squandered an opportunity from God he had prayed for.

Given fear's power to open us up to the "roaring lion," it's no wonder that the Bible tells us to "fear not" more than 300 times!

What should you do when Satan roars at you? Follow the advice found in 1 Peter 5:7:

Casting all your care upon him; for he careth for you.

Put the situation in God's hands by believing and confessing His Word. Then put your faith and trust in His ability to deliver you. Don't fall for the lie that you can't stand against the wiles of the devil. You can! And your spiritual armor is your key to doing so.

Now let's continue looking at the individual pieces of armor and the various deceptions from which they protect you.

The Deception That the Bible Is Not Literally True

In the same survey I mentioned earlier, fewer than 38 percent of Americans affirmed a belief in the accuracy of the Bible.[3] That sad statistic brings us to the first piece of armor described in Ephesians 6:14:

> **Stand therefore, having your loins girt about with truth.**

The following statement might seem overtly obvious, but it needs to be stated plainly: Knowing the truth keeps you from being deceived.

Pretty profound, huh?

This is why, in John 8:31-32, Jesus said,

> **If ye continue in my word, then are ye my disciples indeed; and ye shall know the truth, and the truth shall make you free.**

When you know the truth about something, it guards you from deception in that area and the fear and destruction that deception brings. It is not enough, however, to just generally believe that the Bible is true. You must *know* the Word of truth.

As I heard one preacher say, "Truth itself doesn't set you free; the truth you *know* sets you free."

It is only as you read and study God's Word that you come to know what it says. And knowing what it says provides a standard by which you can measure all concepts, attitudes and ideas—immediately recognizing Satan's lies before they ever have a chance to take root in your heart.

This is why the psalmist said: **Thy word have I hid in mine heart, that I might not sin against thee** (Ps. 119:11).

That, of course, is precisely why Satan tries to deceive you into believing the Bible isn't literally true.

"Oh sure, there might be some good principles to live by in there," he will tell you, "but that book isn't the actual Word of God. Come on, no one believes that anymore!"

But 2 Timothy 3:16-17 plainly says:

All scripture is given by inspiration of God, and is profitable for doctrine, for reproof, for correction, for instruction in righteousness: that the man of God may be perfect, thoroughly furnished unto all good works.

You simply cannot detect and avoid deception if you reject the only source of absolute truth available to mankind.

Think about this for a minute. If whatever you believe about a particular issue doesn't come from the Bible, then the only other possible source for that concept is the human mind. Do you really want to base your life and—more importantly—your eternal destiny on the opinion of some fallen man or woman?

No, me neither.

That is why Satan's undermining your confidence in God's Word is one of his most insidious deceptions.

We must indeed gird our loins with truth.

The Deception That You Are Not Worthy

The next piece of armor God has provided for us is also found in verse 14:

And having put on the breastplate of righteousness...

First, let's define terms. The biblical term *righteousness* simply refers to right-standing before God. It is essentially a judicial term. It connotes the right and ability to stand confidently before a judge or king with no fear of being condemned.

The breastplate of righteousness is important because if you have an unshakable hold on the authority of God's Word, Satan's next ploy will be to convince you that God's promises are true for others but not for you. Why not? Because, he argues, you are not worthy to receive them, of course!

Satan will remind you of everything you have ever done wrong, every unkind word you have ever spoken and every mistake you have ever made—all in an attempt to deceive you into passively accepting the destruction he wants to inject into your life.

Satan wants you to think that you *deserve* sickness, poverty or oppression because of your past. You see, he is fully aware of the truth of 1 John 3:21:

Beloved, if our heart condemn us not, then have we confidence toward God.

Do you see it? The devil's goal in this kind of attack is to rob you of your confidence before God. He knows that if he can make you feel condemned and guilty, you will not as readily resist his advances into your life, because you won't be standing on God's Word in faith. If he is successful in keeping you mindful of past mistakes, you will become like the wretched man described in the first chapter of James:

> **But when he asks, he must believe and not doubt, because he who doubts is like a wave of the sea, blown and tossed by the wind. That man should not think he will receive anything from the Lord; he is a double-minded man, unstable in all he does.**
>
> —JAMES 1:6-8 NIV

This is why the breastplate of righteousness is so vital. A *righteousness consciousness*—as opposed to a *sin consciousness*—protects your heart, just as a literal breastplate does a soldier's.

With a righteousness consciousness, you know that your past doesn't even exist in the eyes of God.

So how does one develop a righteousness consciousness? Or to ask it another way, how does one put on the breastplate of righteousness? It is profoundly simple.

Faith comes by hearing and hearing by the Word of God (Rom. 10:17). And specifically, faith in your right-standing with God comes from meditating on Scriptures such as 2 Corinthians 5:21 (NAS):

He made Him who knew no sin to be sin on our behalf, that we might become the righteousness of God in Him.

God sees you through the sacrifice and blood of Jesus only, and He has given you *His* righteousness—not because of what you have done, but because of what Jesus did for you.

As you can see, one of the most important keys to walking in the fullness of God's promises and blessings is avoiding the "I am not worthy" deception.

That's why it's important to know that your primary defense against this attack is the breastplate of righteousness.

When Satan tries to lie to you about your right-standing with God, just remind him of the power of the blood, and continue to hold on to the righteousness Jesus died to give you.

The Deception That You Are Too Busy To Work for God

Moving down to verse 15 of Ephesians chapter 6, we find the next piece of deception-repelling armor:

...And your feet shod with the preparation of the gospel of peace.

God's plan for you in this life involves using all the resources with which He has entrusted you to spread the gospel of peace. You put on this piece of armor when you make it your determined purpose to let God use you to bring His power into someone's life through the gospel.

The deception you must be on guard against is allowing the enemy to convince you that your other priorities don't leave room for carrying out what Paul calls our ministry of reconciliation. (2 Cor. 5:18.)

Instead of using your finances to support someone's ministry, using your time to share your faith with a co-worker or simply letting your neighbors know whom you live for, Satan will labor to refocus your attention on advancing your career, acquiring some new material object or climbing the social ladder.

If the devil can get you to fill your life with your own pursuits, he will have succeeded in getting your eyes off meeting other people's needs. You will focus solely on taking care of your agenda.

But if you fall into this deception, you won't consistently pursue God's plan for your life, you will be little or no threat to Satan's kingdom and you will never even come close to experiencing God's highest and best.

Now, here is an important biblical truth that will change your life if you will embrace it: *God always dispenses His power in accordance with His purposes. And His highest purpose is to save the lost and dying among us.*

I frequently talk to people who say that they want to see more of God's power operating in their lives. They see God moving powerfully on the behalf of other believers and want to experience the same level of miraculous blessing themselves.

Upon further investigation, I often discover that these people spend very little time, money or effort getting the gospel out to the lost world. I then have to point out to them that they are expecting God to dispense His power outside of His purpose—something He will never do.

If you want to see more of God's power operating in your life, then align your life with His higher purpose. Start using the resources He has given you to facilitate the spread of the gospel. The degree to which you do this is the degree to which you will see miracles flowing in your life.

I've heard a common saying in business circles that is so true: No man on his deathbed ever wished he had spent more time at the office.

The regrets that come at the end of life invariably center on the neglect of eternal things. Having your feet shod with the preparation of the gospel of peace helps to keep you from falling for a deception that would rob you of the power of God and the joy that comes from fulfilling your highest destiny.

The Deception That It Doesn't Matter What You Believe

Your enemy knows that the Bible says, **As** [a man] **thinketh in his heart, so is he** (Prov. 23:7). He knows that what you believe directly affects the decisions you make. So if he can get you to believe something other than God's Word, he can get you to inadvertently choose the results of the curse rather than redemption and blessing.

This is why the Bible places special emphasis on your next piece of armor:

Above all, taking the shield of faith, wherewith ye shall be able to quench all the fiery darts of the wicked.

—EPHESIANS 6:16

Satan also knows that without faith it is impossible to please God and that a double-minded man will receive nothing from the Lord. (Heb. 11:6; James 1:7,8.) So he will do all he can to get you to waver every time you take a stand on God's Word.

It is important to understand that in this present age, Satan is still operating as the ruler of this fallen world. As such, he has some rights and ability to manipulate people and circumstances. You can be sure that he will do so in such a way as to contradict what you are believing. He will try to make it look as if God's Word isn't true or your faith isn't working. The goal is to get you to waver in your beliefs.

Satan desperately hopes that you will let down your shield of faith. He knows that God designed it to protect you from his fiery darts of doubt and wavering unbelief—the things that keep you from experiencing the full manifestation of God's promises.

Keep that shield held high, and stand firm in your faith. And nothing in this world will be able to affect what you believe and thus stop you from receiving God's promises.

If you don't quit believing, you win. To become convinced otherwise is a tragic deception.

The Deception That It Doesn't Matter What You Think

Another deception the devil uses is against the mind. That's why Ephesians 6:17 refers to putting on your **helmet of salvation.**

Metaphorically speaking, a helmet covers the mind. Obviously, your mind is Satan's primary target in his efforts to deceive you. That is why it is vital that you protect your mind by **...casting down imaginations, and every high thing that exalteth itself against the knowledge of God, and bringing into captivity every thought to the obedience of Christ** (2 Cor. 10:5).

Why are thoughts so important? Because your imagination will eventually produce corresponding behavior. Let me give you an example of this. In Genesis 11, we find the account of the people building the tower of Babel, in which God says,

> **And now nothing will be restrained from them, which they have imagined to do.**
>
> —GENESIS 11:6

Like it or not, your capacity to imagine your life being a certain way supernaturally affects the direction it ultimately takes. Thoughts have consequences.

If you want your life to be the way God says it should be, then you need to think as God thinks and imagine your life the way God sees it.

Satan, of course, wants you to be casual about your thought life. He hopes that you won't pay much attention to the thoughts you entertain in your mind. He will tell you that your thoughts are harmless. He will whisper that they don't really matter because nobody can tell what you are thinking anyway.

Don't let Satan deceive you concerning the importance of your thoughts. For example, letting thoughts of anger, hatred, resentment or unforgiveness stay in your mind will hinder and ultimately destroy your ability to walk in love. Without love, your faith won't work. (Gal. 5:6.) And without faith it is impossible to please God or walk in His blessings. (Heb. 11:1-6.)

Harboring thoughts of lust, for another example, will inevitably lead to the breakdown of your resistance to acting out those imaginations. Spend enough time mentally seeing yourself doing something, and before long, actually *doing* it will be easy. Many people who never dreamed themselves capable of committing terrible acts nonetheless find themselves committing them simply because they spent enough time thinking about it.

Remember, nobody will restrain you from doing the things you imagine. *You* must cast down those vain imaginations and ungodly thoughts and replace them with God's thoughts.

"But Mac," you may be asking, "how can I know what God's thoughts are?"

That's easy; He has written them down for you in His Word. And as you find out what the Word says, use the helmet of salvation to protect yourself from this deadly deception.

The Deception That It Doesn't Matter What You Say

The philosopher Jean-Paul Sartre once said, "Words are loaded pistols."[4] He was right, and that brings us to the next area in which deception is so deadly: your words.

The final piece of armor mentioned in Ephesians 6 is the piece God's given us to defend ourselves from this particular deception. Notice that it differs from all the others in that it is actually an *offensive* weapon:

> **And take...the sword of the Spirit, which is the word of God.**
>
> —EPHESIANS 6:17

Just as Satan wants you to be casual about your thoughts, so he also wants you to be about your words. Actually, the two are connected; wrong thoughts invariably lead to wrong words, and as the Bible says in Proverbs 18:21, **Death and life are in the power of the tongue.**

According to Hebrews 11, the words you speak today frame the world you will step into tomorrow, because your words are containers of your faith. Your words are the "change agents" you speak out to shape your world around you. Mark 11:23 says that you will have **whatsoever you** *say.*

Satan knows that this principle will work *for* you or *against* you, depending on what kind of words are coming out of your mouth.

That is why it is vital never to mindlessly articulate the negative circumstances you encounter. In other words, don't go around saying, "I'm feeling sick. I must be coming down with something" or "I'm going broke. We'll probably lose the house" and so forth. When you do so, you actually come into agreement with Satan, and your own words open the door for him to bring to pass in your life whatever you've said.

I urge you to examine your vocabulary. Listen to your words and guard your mouth. You can't afford to allow your own tongue to speak curses and death into your life.

Right words are absolutely critical to attaining God's plan for your life. Never be deceived into thinking you can be casual about them, but don't let Satan tell you that you don't need to speak positive, faith-filled words about your-self either. You do!

Satan is an enemy who will never quit trying to hinder you any way he can. He wants to push you away from God and destroy you, but he will settle for preventing you from making any further progress toward God's destiny for your life. But he can't stop you if you keep speaking God's Word instead of careless words.

The Word of God in your mouth is a mighty sword. Wield it well.

The Deception That You Can't "Pray Always"

This passage describing the armor of the believer ends significantly: It closes with a word about prayer.

Praying always with all prayer and supplication in the Spirit, and watching thereunto with all perseverance and supplication for all saints.

—EPHESIANS 6:18

Praying always. Seems like a pretty tall order, doesn't it? Impossible even? That is precisely what the enemy hopes you will think.

You see, your prayer life is an area in which Satan uses busyness to deceive you. He will labor overtime to convince you that prayer is unimportant or a luxury you simply can't afford. He will see to it that there are a multitude of tasks to which you need to attend—all of which seem to take priority over prayer.

The devil will tell you, *You can't pray all day. You have business to do, a house to clean and children to care for.*

But prayer, in the sense implied in verse 18, simply means a continual awareness of the presence of God in our everyday lives. It is what Brother Lawrence has called "practicing the presence of God."[5]

"Praying always" does not mean spending all day on your knees. It is simply maintaining your communion with the Greater One who lives in you. Don't let Satan use a false concept of God's expectations to keep you from spending time with your heavenly Father and staying connected with your only source of life.

Armor-Plated Living

In summary, the following arguments are the most common forms of deception used by the enemy of your soul:

You are too busy to pray.

The words you speak don't have any real significance.

Nobody knows what you are thinking, so you can feel secure in that privacy and let your thoughts run wild.

It doesn't matter what you believe. You can't control the circumstances in your life anyway.

You have more important things to do than share your faith and help spread the gospel.

You are not good enough for God to bless you.

The Bible might have worked at one time, but it is not really applicable in today's society.

Satan is too powerful for you anyway. Others might be able to handle him, but you had better not make him mad at you or else he will really come after you.

Satan is not your problem; it is all these awful people around you. If they would just do what you want, everything would be fine.

Do any of these lies sound familiar? Satan uses them all the time. But by consistently putting on the whole armor of God, you close some significant doorways to deception in your life. These aren't, however, the only doorways the devil uses. In the following chapters, we will explore some other deceptions the enemy uses to keep believers from experiencing all the wonderful things God has for His children.

For now, simply plant this truth firmly in your heart: Satan cannot defeat you in any area of your life unless he can first deceive you. And one of the primary defenses God has given us against deception is the whole armor of God.

CHAPTER 3

The actions of men are the best interpreters of their thoughts.

—John Locke[1]

Being "All Ears"

In the first chapter of James, the Word of God reveals a major doorway through which Satan can come to deceive us. Verse 22 says,

But be ye doers of the word, and not hearers only, deceiving your own selves.

Every time God quickens some portion of the Word of God to your heart and you fail—or refuse—to act on it, you leave a door wide open for Satan to enter your life with some form of darkness. In fact, this verse indicates that in such a case you are actually the agent of your own deception!

You see, every time you fail to act on the Word, you are saying by your actions something you would probably never say with your lips: *I don't believe God's Word is true, and I have a better plan.*

At that point the devil's work has been done for him. He doesn't need to sow doubt in your heart about the authority of God's Word and the truth of His promises—you have done it yourself. You have actually made it easier for Satan to bring the effects of the curse into that area of your life because he doesn't have to overcome your faith in that Word.

As James 2:17 declares, **Faith, if it hath not without works** [corresponding action], **is dead.** Thus, with no shield of faith positioned between you and Satan, you become easy prey.

Yes, **faith cometh by hearing, and hearing by the word of God** (Rom. 10:17). But without your corresponding action, that faith is powerless to help you. In fact, the word translated "hearers" in James 1:22 is similar to the Greek word translated "hearing" in Romans 10:17.[2]

So James is not necessarily talking about hearing with your natural ears but rather hearing with your heart, which is precisely how faith comes. Yet by not *doing* that Word, you can still be deceived.

This form of deception has a close relative. It comes when Satan is able to plug people's spiritual ears with religious tradition.

Deafness by Tradition

Jesus told the religious leaders of His day—the scribes and the Pharisees—that their traditions had made the Word of God ineffectual:

> **Thus have ye made the commandment of God of none effect by your tradition.**
>
> —MATTHEW 15:6

Since the Word of God is intended to bring the awesome force of faith to bear on your circumstances, Jesus is saying here that the tradition of man will stop faith from coming.

Why? Because those bound up in tradition don't have ears to hear what the Spirit of God is saying.

People steeped in religious (as opposed to scriptural) thinking have no capacity to receive revelation knowledge from the Word. As a result, faith can't come to them.

Jesus defined tradition as the **commandments of men** (Matt. 15:9). You will find that such commandments have no solid root in the Word of God and often even contradict Scripture.

A good example would be a doctrine taught by many churches—one that proclaims being sprinkled as an infant makes your salvation secure as an adult. Those who hold to that tradition have a difficult time embracing the truth of Jesus' words in John 3—that they must be born again. They simply don't have ears to hear that vital truth because their tradition keeps them from hearing it.

Still, there are many others who hear the Word of God, believe it and yet won't do it!

I believe that the Lord has shown me three reasons why many believers *hear* but don't *do* His Word, even though they truly believe that it would be best for them to obey it.

The Barrier of Lust

The first reason is simply the resistance created by something the Bible calls the lust of the flesh. Lust is any powerful desire of the flesh. Most people usually attach a sexual connotation to the word, but it really encompasses anything your flesh strongly craves.

Addictive behavior is a form of lust that illustrates this truth quite well. I am sure there is not one Christian who is addicted to drugs, alcohol or cigarettes who doesn't know deep down in his spirit that he is slowly killing himself.

Such people may even believe what the Word says about the body being the temple of the Holy Ghost, that it is to be presented as a living sacrifice to God. Still, for most the desire is so powerful they can't overcome it.

Not all lust is physical, however. Unforgiveness can be a lust; Christians may hold on to a grudge and refuse to forgive someone who hurt them because it feels good to their flesh to nurse their bitter feelings. They may want to try to repay the wrong that was done, even though they know in their hearts that they are to walk in love and forgive as Christ forgave them.

Selfishness is another area in which people's flesh can give them trouble. If, for example, they have received the revelation that they should give tithes but have other things they want to do with that money to satisfy their flesh, then the cravings of the flesh may keep them from being doers of the Word.

The Barrier of Fear

The second reason people don't do the Word is fear—or perhaps I should say more specifically, the fear of man.

God has called all of us to share the gospel, lay hands on the sick and in general reach out to the lost as ministers of reconciliation. But most Christians simply won't tell folks what Jesus has done for them because they are afraid of being mocked, rejected or persecuted.

Many don't walk in love because they are fearful of being hurt in some way. And how many millions are missing out on the blessings of the baptism in the Holy Spirit simply because they are afraid of what their families and other church members might think?

Untold numbers of Christians are not doers of the Word simply because of fear.

The Barrier of Time

The third and possibly most prevalent reason for not doing the Word is procrastination.

If you have ever said, "Yes, Lord, I will do what I see Your Word says about this—tomorrow," then you have fallen for this deception. It is always easier to say, "I will quit smoking tomorrow," or "I plan to start tithing next month," or "I will go out witnessing next week." The problem is, you will always have a seemingly good reason to put off being obedient.

The Amplified Bible's rendering of James 1:22 makes it more clear as to how this happens. It says,

> **Be doers of the Word [obey the message], and not merely listeners to it, betraying yourselves [into deception by reasoning contrary to the Truth].**

When a sincere believer fails to act on the Word, his conscience begins to bother him. In order to silence that guilty conscience, he must engage in something called self-justification (or, as the verse we just read calls it, "reasoning contrary to the Truth").

Such a person says, "I can't do that now because..." and then gives some rationalization that keeps him from feeling too bad about it.

The moment you do that, you open a door of deception that Satan quickly uses as an entry point to bring negative situations into your life and home.

These things seldom become evident overnight, however, and so the longer you reason against the truth, the more comfortable you become with deception. By the time the seeds of destruction begin sprouting in your life, you may not make the connection between your failure to act on the Word and the harvest of destruction you are presently reaping.

That is when Christians find themselves asking questions such as these: *Why is this happening to me? Maybe this faith stuff doesn't really work all the time. Is God trying to teach me something? Did I do something to make Him angry with me?*

And thus the deception grows deeper.

The belief that you can consistently hear the Word and yet fail to act on it without experiencing some negative consequences is a serious form of deception.

How To Do the Word

"All right, Pastor," you might be saying at this point, "I can see that I need to close this doorway to deception by acting on the Word that I hear. But, come on—this is easier said than done. Just how *do* I deal with lust, fear, selfishness and procrastination?"

Without a doubt, psychologically or chemically addictive behaviors, selfishness, fear and a tendency to rationalize can be powerful forces in people's lives. Even secular studies demonstrate that most people change these kinds of behaviors only with great difficulty, if at all.

We can also see from the results of these studies that trying to exercise greater willpower or self-control is not going to effect permanent changes in most people's lives. (The 10-percent long-term success rate of most government drug rehabilitation programs clearly bears that out.)

As always, the answer to this conundrum is found in the Word of God—in this case in Ephesians 1:18-19:

> **The eyes of your understanding being enlightened; that ye may know what is the hope of his calling, and what the riches of the glory of his inheritance in the saints, and what is the exceeding greatness of his power to us-ward who believe, according to the working of his mighty power.**

The same power that raised Christ Jesus from the dead is certainly more than enough to overcome any paralyzing fear or contrary behavior in our lives.

I should say here that since none of us has achieved perfection, until Jesus returns we all have to deal with these issues from time to time. What you must learn to do is not just exercise your willpower, but rather tap into the power that is available **to us-ward who believe.**

Don't ever let Satan deceive you into thinking that your faith isn't important. When you are among those who believe, great power is available to you.

How do you tap into that power? Let's go back to James 1:22 and read on to verse 25 to find the answer:

But be ye doers of the word, and not hearers only, deceiving your own selves. For if any be a hearer of the word, and not a doer, he is like unto a man beholding his natural face in a glass: for he beholdeth himself, and goeth his way, and straightway forgetteth what manner of man he was. But whoso looketh into the perfect law of liberty, and continueth therein, he being not a forgetful hearer, but a doer of the work, this man shall be blessed in his deed.

In verses 24 and 25, the Greek words translated "forgetteth" and "forgetful" literally mean "to lose out of mind by neglect."[3] Here it tells you that if you are going to be a doer of the Word, then you are going to have to do something about what is in your mind.

Verse 25 says, **Being not a forgetful hearer but a doer.** We are hearers of what? We are hearers of the **perfect law of liberty,** or in other words, God's Word. Thus, it could say, "Being not a forgetful hearer of God's Word, but a doer."

Add the Greek definition of *forgetful* and you have, "not putting out of mind God's Word, but being a doer." Or to say it yet another way, "Keeping God's Word in your mind and being a doer of the Word."

Bridle That Tongue

Now let's look at the next key to doing the Word. We find it in the very next verse:

**If any man among you seem to be religious, and
bridleth not his tongue, but deceiveth his own heart,
this man's religion is vain.**

—JAMES 1:26

Here the Bible warns us of another source of deception
besides that of hearing the Word and not doing it. Now it
adds this truth: If you think you have it all together spiritually but don't keep your tongue from speaking things
contrary to God's Word, then you are fooling yourself.

Does this sound familiar? Remember, the verses in
Ephesians we looked at in the previous chapter showed us
that Satan will try to deceive us into believing our thoughts
and words are inconsequential. But don't we all eventually
say what we have been thinking? Jesus said we do:

**A good man out of the good treasure of his heart
bringeth forth that which is good; and an evil man
out of the evil treasure of his heart bringeth forth
that which is evil: for of the abundance of the heart
his mouth speaketh.**

—LUKE 6:45

The two principal factors that determine whether or not
you become a doer of the Word are what you think on and
what you speak. If you meditate on God's Word and then
speak God's Word, you will tap into **the exceeding greatness
of his power to us-ward who believe.** And that power can
and will change your behavior. You *will* become a doer of
the Word—not by your own strength and resolve but by the
power of God that resides in His Word.

Let me show you the same truth in another Scripture. There are many places in the Bible that confirm this truth, but in Joshua 1:8 God plainly tells us how to *do* the Word. Keep in mind that if it worked for Joshua, it will work for us. God is no respecter of persons. He recorded this for our benefit as well:

This book of the law shall not depart out of thy mouth; but thou shalt meditate therein day and night, that thou mayest observe to do according to all that is written therein: [Why?] for then thou shalt make thy way prosperous, and then thou shalt have good success.

Notice this verse says you observe, or *do,* the law (God's Word) only after you have meditated on it and spoken it.

Consistent *doing* is always preceded by consistent *thinking* and consistent *speaking*. Now notice something else about what God told Joshua: Thinking the Word, speaking the Word and then doing the Word lead to being prosperous and having good success.

Failure to do the Word, however, leads to deception. And as we have seen, deception leads to something very different from prosperity and success.

Think It, Speak It, Do It

In the previous chapter, we looked at the need to cast down vain imaginations. However, the principle of thinking, speaking and doing is so vitally important to all of us that I need to expand upon it even further here.

You have the God-given capacity to imagine, or mentally picture, experiencing your life in a particular way. The way you see your life has a big impact on how you experience it. This isn't magic; it is simply that your imagination tends to prompt and motivate your behavior.

This is why Satan wants you to have vain—empty and foolish—imaginations. He wants you to fantasize about sinful things. The devil wants you to see yourself defeated, sick and broke. He wants you to think only about yourself and your needs. Why? He does so because as you dwell on those kinds of thoughts, they influence the direction of your life.

If you are in difficult straits now, Satan will try to keep you there by promoting vain imaginations consistent with that negative situation. Let me remind you again of what the Word says in this matter: **As** [a man] **thinketh in his heart, so is he** (Prov. 23:7).

Don't let thoughts contrary to God's Word stay in your mind. Cast down vain thoughts and bring them captive to the obedience of Christ. Begin imagining yourself doing mighty works for God. See yourself as being more than a conqueror and able to do all things through Christ who strengthens you.

Pray in the Holy Spirit, and yield your life to His ministry. And as 1 Corinthians 2:9 promises, God will show you things your eye hasn't seen, your ear hasn't heard and your heart hasn't even pondered. He will show you what He has prepared for those who love Him.

Not only can you imagine the promises in God's Word being fully operative in your life, but you can also receive a grand image or vision from the Holy Spirit of what God has specifically planned for you.

As you meditate on God's plan for your life and begin to talk about that plan, you will begin tapping into that exceeding greatness of His power. And the things in your life that would stand in the way of God's purpose for you will begin to fall away.

The Word further promises that you will be delivered and set free from all of Satan's hindrances. But most importantly, you will become a doer of the things you have heard and believed. And when that happens, it closes a major door to deception in your life and you can begin to become all that God intends you to be.

CHAPTER 4

Worldliness is a spirit, a temperament, an attitude of the soul. It is a life without high callings, life devoid of lofty ideals. It is a gaze always horizontal and never vertical.

The Samson Syndrome

—John Henry Jowett[1]

It comes with the territory: Because we each live in a body of flesh and that flesh wants to experience the pleasures this world has to offer, we have a tendency to be drawn toward what the world holds up to us as enjoyment and fulfillment.

But that's deception.

We all want to be accepted and loved by others. We want to take part in what we perceive to be "the good life." This is why we must keep our flesh under control and base our perception of what constitutes the good life solely on God's Word.

I want to show you a powerful example of a mighty man of God who, through his love for the things of the world, fell into deception and was ultimately destroyed. That man was Samson, and through his life we can learn some things that can keep us from making similar mistakes.

In chapter 16 of Judges, we find the spectacular but sad story of Samson's death.

Then the lords of the Philistines gathered them together for to offer a great sacrifice unto Dagon

their god, and to rejoice: for they said, Our god hath delivered Samson our enemy into our hand. And when the people saw him, they praised their god: for they said, Our god hath delivered into our hands our enemy, and the destroyer of our country, which slew many of us.

And it came to pass, when their hearts were merry, that they said, Call for Samson, that he may make us sport. And they called for Samson out of the prison house; and he made them sport: and they set him between the pillars. And Samson said unto the lad that held him by the hand, Suffer me that I may feel the pillars whereupon the house standeth, that I may lean upon them.

Now the house was full of men and women; and all the lords of the Philistines were there; and there were upon the roof about three thousand men and women, that beheld while Samson made sport. And Samson called unto the Lord, and said, O Lord God, remember me, I pray thee, and strengthen me, I pray thee, only this once, O God, that I may be at once avenged of the Philistines for my two eyes. [The Philistines had blinded Samson when they took him captive.]

And Samson took hold of the two middle pillars upon which the house stood, and on which it was borne up, of the one with his right hand, and of the other with his left. And Samson said, Let me die with the Philistines. And he bowed himself with all his might; and the house fell upon the lords, and upon all the people that were therein. So the dead which he slew at his death were more than they which he slew in his life.

—JUDGES 16:23-30

In the past some teachers have used this passage to make the point that God's justice always triumphs and that no matter how bad the situation looks, you can always come out on top in God. That is a wonderful truth, but it is not the lesson I take away from this account.

If you study Samson's life in chapters 13 through 16, you see that the Spirit of the Lord moved mightily throughout his life with manifestations of supernatural strength.

So what did Samson, who once slew 1000 Philistines with the jawbone of a donkey, do wrong? How did he end up being captured, chained, blinded and then mocked and humiliated?

Although Samson wrought a great victory for God at his death, he nonetheless died prematurely. So why did Samson, an anointed deliverer of the children of God, only rule Israel as a judge for twenty years? Why did Samson die so young?

If you have read the story, you know that the answer to these questions is deception—deception in the form of a woman named Delilah. I am convinced God recorded this story to illustrate the consequences of opening a door to deception.

It is important to understand that Samson had a special covenant with God. As a Nazarite, he had vowed not to touch any unclean thing, partake of wine or strong drink or cut his hair. (You can read about the Nazarite covenant in Numbers 6:1-21.)

If the part about Samson's hair strikes you as peculiar, you need to know that hair is often used in the Bible as a type of the glory of God. Samson's hair was to be a statement to all who saw him that the presence and glory of God was on his life. His vow not to cut it represented the priority and importance of that covenant of glory.

Fellowship With the World

Samson's first mistake is recorded in Judges 14, when he moves to a Philistine city—which is a type of the world—and marries a Philistine woman.

This action is today equivalent to a believer's becoming unequally yoked with an unbeliever. In the context of God's laws and his Nazarite vow, Samson's new bride actually defiled him and made him unclean.

In chapter 14, verse 10, the Bible tells us that Samson made a feast in that Philistine city. The Hebrew word translated "feast" is used in other parts of the Bible to refer to a meal in which alcohol is consumed. We can infer from this text that the friendlier Samson became with the world, the more his fidelity to his vows eroded.

By the time we reach chapter 16, Samson has gone to Gaza, another Philistine city, where he sleeps with a harlot. And from there he is off to yet another Philistine city, where he falls in love with a Philistine woman named Delilah. Delilah is of course the woman who cut Samson's hair, thereby defeating him.

Now, if you didn't read the whole account, you might think that Samson was just an unfortunate victim of Delilah's deception. But the Scriptures make it clear that his fidelity to his vow had gone by the wayside long before.

You see, Samson liked to drink and party in the enemy's cities. He was promiscuous and eventually fell in love with Delilah, a worldly woman. Yet a measure of the anointing of God was still present in his life. Throughout all this, he was still doing mighty works for God.

No doubt Samson's parents objected to his behavior. But I can almost hear what he was thinking while listening to them: *Yes, I know I am not supposed to do these things. I know I have broken my vow. But, hey, it doesn't seem to have hurt anything. The anointing is still present. I am still doing great things for God!*

The magnitude of that deception should be obvious. Don't ever let yourself think that simply because God is still using you to promote His plan, He condones your compromising with the world. You are just experiencing God's great mercy. God is long-suffering; He will extend the opportunity to repent as long as He can. But the day always comes when, just as for Samson, the consequences of one's actions become manifest.

Eventually, the chickens always come home to roost, as they say.

It hurts me to say it, but I know there are many in the body of Christ who have fallen into this trap of rationalizing. They will tell you, "It's not really *that* bad we are sleeping together, because we are engaged and getting married soon. We just wanted to make sure we're sexually compatible."

What produces that kind of deception? It starts when you let yourself be drawn into the world. It comes when you begin to pursue the things of the world and adopt the fallen values of the world system. How do you prevent it? Heed God's warning in 1 John 2:15:

Love not the world, neither the things that are in the world. If any man love the world, the love of the Father is not in him.

It might surprise you to learn the Greek word translated "love" here is *agape*. Although *agape* usually refers to the God-kind of love, its root meaning is "to give."[2] This verse says you are not to give yourself to the world or the things in the world, because if you do, you won't give yourself to the pursuit of God.

It will also help you to know that the word for "world" in this verse is *kosmos,* which usually refers to social systems or social orders.[3] Here it refers to the way the world works and its value system.

The problem with the world is that it doesn't really have a value system. The world will tell you, "Go ahead. Do whatever you think is right for you, as long as you don't hurt anybody else."

That sounds good to the flesh, because then it can have pretty much anything it wants. The trouble is, your carnal nature doesn't understand the concept of consequences. It just wants to feel good. Thus it will lead you down a path to deception and death every time.

My dear friend, please understand something about worldly temptations. They always hold out a promise of immediate rewards while minimizing or rationalizing away the long-term consequences.

"Go ahead, have a beer or two," is the worldly rationalization. "You will get to hang out with these really cool people. You will make some great new friends and have a really good time tonight. Don't worry about your relationship with God. You can always repent tomorrow. Who knows? Maybe you will get a chance to share the gospel with them after you have gotten to know them better."

Or maybe it goes something like this: "You know, you could take advantage of that great deal on the stereo you have always wanted if you just used this month's tithe for it. If you wait, you will miss out and you won't ever get a deal like that again. Besides, you can make up your tithe next month. God will understand. He wants you to have good stuff, right?"

I could go on, but I am sure you see the pattern. Please keep in mind that God is not against your having things. In fact, **He giveth us richly all things to enjoy** (1 Tim. 6:17). But that's only if we make Him the focus of our trust.

After all, God created this earth for our enjoyment and blessing. Just don't give yourself to the pursuit of the world and its things, or you won't be able to give yourself wholly to the pursuit of God.

Closing the Door

From Samson's experience it should be clear that you need to close the door to all ungodly relationships in your life. Don't let worldly people have any input into your life. The Bible says it plainly:

And what concord hath Christ with Belial? or what part hath he that believeth with an infidel? And what agreement hath the temple of God with idols? for ye are the temple of the living God; as God hath said, I will dwell in them, and walk in them; and I will be their God, and they shall be my people. Wherefore come out from among them, and be ye separate, saith the Lord, and touch not the unclean thing; and I will receive you.

—2 CORINTHIANS 6:15-17

I know that this may seem harsh, but according to this verse not only are you not to fellowship with unbelievers, you are also to avoid those who profess to be Christians but who live ungodly lives. If they claim to love and serve God but are busy doing what the world does, then something is very wrong. We just read in 1 John 2 that you can't love (give yourself to) God *and* the world.

Sure, one might get away with flouting these principles for a while. But eventually the day of accounting will come, and let me tell you, the kingdom of darkness is a hard taskmaster. If you allow yourself to be deceived by worldly rationalizations, then just like Samson, you will be deceived, blinded and taken captive by the enemy of your soul.

Now I can almost hear you saying, "Well, Pastor Mac, I can see the truth about the danger of ungodly fellowship, but *my* old friends are all right. They aren't bad people basically. I will just be more careful when I am around them from now on."

No, you won't. Read Judges 16:4-21. Even after Delilah tried to betray him three times, Samson didn't end the relationship. He still opened his heart to her, and she succeeded in betraying him the fourth time when she cut his hair. But this time, something different happened. Look at verses 20 and 21:

> **So he [Samson] awoke from his sleep, and said, "I will go out as before, at other times, and shake myself free!" But he did not know that the Lord had departed from him. Then the Philistines took him and put out his eyes, and brought him down to Gaza. They bound him with bronze fetters, and he became a grinder in the prison** (NKJV).

Can you see how Samson took God's anointing for granted? He had ample opportunity to escape destruction. Doesn't it appear as if Samson treated the whole thing as some sort of game? Why didn't he see the danger that is so obvious to us as we read about it today?

I can answer those questions in one word—*deception*. It was deception brought about by his desire for an ungodly relationship. You simply cannot compromise your covenant as a way of life and expect to be led by the Spirit of God or experience His anointing.

Now, I am not saying you should burn all of your relational bridges the day you get saved. Not at all. God may indeed use you to speak into the lives of your past friends, to plant the Word of God in their hearts and help them get saved. And by all means love them and pray for them.

But that doesn't mean you should fellowship with them. You can't allow an impartation of the world's lifestyle to infiltrate yours. You just can't open your heart to them. Haggai makes it clear that holiness is not infectious, but unhappiness is. (Hag. 2:11-13.)

Closing the door to the influences of the world also involves making sure the number-one priority in your life is loving and serving God.

You must examine the priorities you have set in your life. What is your number-one goal? What do you spend the most time pursuing? What plans in your schedule do you never cancel? How are you using your money? Are the resources of your life being used to pursue something *you* want, or are you seeking to promote God's plan? Are you loving—giving yourself to—the world and its pursuits, or are you loving—giving yourself to—God and His pursuits?

If you will make knowing, loving and serving God with all of your life's resources—your time, talent and money—your top priority, then by the hand of God, good things will come. You will close the door to the deception of loving the world, or the Samson syndrome. And Satan will no longer be able to use the people and things of this world to deceive you.

CHAPTER 5

O thou invisible spirit of wine, if thou hast no name to be known by, let us call thee devil!

—William Shakespeare[1]

The Deception of Alcohol

There's another issue on the subject of deception that I must address, although it does not fit within the primary scope or focus of this book. I feel strongly led to bring up this issue because it concerns a source of deception that produces much unnecessary pain and heartache in the Body of Christ: the deception of alcohol.

In chapter 4, "The Samson Syndrome," we saw how Samson's love for the world deceived and ultimately destroyed a great man of God. We saw in Samson's example the deceptive power of drinking and partying.

Sadly, there is much confusion in the Body of Christ today over whether or not it is acceptable for a believer to drink alcoholic beverages. Because of that confusion, I feel that I *must* address this issue.

You see, knowing what the Bible says about the kind of deception that the love of the world—in this case, drinking—brings, it grieves me to know there are ministers out there teaching Christians that drinking is, at worst, a morally neutral activity.

I am not going to beat around the bush or be "politically correct" on this issue. If you think you can drink socially without hurting your effectiveness for God, you are deceived and you have left a door wide open for Satan.

Let me ask you a few questions: Is not alcohol a mind-altering substance? Does it not affect one's judgment? Doesn't alcohol change an individual into a different person intellectually and emotionally? Are not people who are "under the influence" dangerous to themselves and others? Do you think that it is okay to do a little crack or marijuana or heroin? Are they not, like alcohol, also mind-altering substances? Do you let your children drink?

What makes you think God will tell His children it is okay to partake of something that has destroyed countless millions of lives, families and yes, even ministries? Alcohol is nothing less than Satan's counterfeit of the new wine of the Holy Ghost that was poured out at Pentecost. On that day, Peter announced,

These are not drunken as ye suppose.

—ACTS 2:15

If you have experienced being intoxicated both in the Holy Spirit and with alcohol, then you understand that Satan's version is a very poor copy of the real thing. One brings refreshment, joy and life; the other slowly poisons your body while deceiving you into thinking that you are having a good time.

Just what *does* God have to say about alcohol? Let's look at Proverbs 23:29-33:

Who hath woe? who hath sorrow? who hath
contentions? who hath babbling? who hath wounds
without cause? who hath redness of eyes? They that
tarry long at the wine; they that go to seek mixed
wine. Look not thou upon the wine when it is red,
when it giveth his colour in the cup, when it moveth
itself aright. At the last it biteth like a serpent, and
stingeth like an adder. Thine eyes shall behold strange
women, and thine heart shall utter perverse things.

Was it not a strange woman that was the instrument of
Samson's destruction?

Verses 34 and 35 continue:

Yea, thou shalt be as he that lieth down in the
midst of the sea, or as he that lieth upon the top of a
mast. They have stricken me, shalt thou say, and I
was not sick; they have beaten me, and I felt it not:
when shall I awake? I will seek it yet again.

Verse 31 makes it clear that these Scriptures are clearly
talking about alcohol. Wine changes color and bubbles up
when it is fermented. Here God is not just telling us not to
drink it, but also not to even look at it.

Why? He gives us that command because it damages
your life and causes you to go back to it again and again.

A New Testament passage, Luke 1, speaks quite plainly
about this issue. There we find the angel Gabriel speaking to
Zacharias about his coming son, John the Baptist.

But the angel said unto him, Fear not, Zacharias:
for thy prayer is heard; and thy wife Elisabeth shall

bear thee a son, and thou shalt call his name John. And thou shalt have joy and gladness; and many shall rejoice at his birth. For he shall be great in the sight of the Lord, and shall drink neither wine nor strong drink; and he shall be filled with the Holy Ghost, even from his mother's womb.

And many of the children of Israel shall he turn to the Lord their God. And he shall go before him in the spirit and power of Elias, to turn the hearts of the fathers to the children, and the disobedient to the wisdom of the just; to make ready a people prepared for the Lord.

It is no small thing that the Bible tells us John would not touch wine or strong drink and then immediately reveals that he would be filled with the Holy Spirit from the womb.

You, as a born-again child of God, are also filled with the same Holy Spirit and power of God. So similarly, you need not touch wine or strong drink.

Let me ask you another question. Do you think God will allow His power—the power that created this universe and raised Jesus from the dead—to flow through a vessel that is impaired by alcohol or any other drug, even a little bit? God is saying here that His anointing and alcohol will not mix in the same vessel.

Do you see how we must interpret the Word of God in the context of God's big picture and plan for us? God is not about to suggest it is all right for His children to partake of even a bit of anything that has the capacity to deceive and eventually destroy them.

I encourage you to do a word study on the word *wine*. As you study all of the Scriptures that talk about wine, ask the Lord to reveal the truth of His Word to you concerning alcohol. And slam this door to deception in the face of the devil for you and your family forever!

CHAPTER 6

Churchgoers are like coals of fire. When they cling together, they keep the flame aglow; when they separate, they die out.

Division

—Billy Graham[1]

Another major doorway to deception Satan tries to use to gain entrance into our lives is one that I call "the doorway of division." When I say *division,* I am talking about being divided from the unique place in the Body of Christ in which God has set you.

Is there such a place? you may be thinking. I will answer that question by pointing you to an interesting passage of Scripture in which we find two apostles being detained by religious leaders for working a miracle and preaching about Jesus:

> And being let go, they went to *their own company,* and reported all that the chief priests and elders had said unto them.
>
> —ACTS 4:23

Here in Acts 4 we see Peter and John returning not just to any company, but to their own company. It was there they all prayed with such power that the place was shaken. There they all were filled with boldness, and there none experienced any kind of lack.

God tells us in 1 Corinthians 12:18 that He places every member in the body as it pleases Him. It is important to realize that God has a specific place for you in the Body of Christ—a place in which you can receive from Him all you need to grow in faith and prosper in every area of your life, a place in which your supply of time, talent and finances are most needed to enable the Body to be built up and to increase in influence.

Anything that would move you from that place is divisive and rooted in deception. Just as it is important for your hand to be connected to your body, so you need likewise to remain connected to the place in the Body of Christ in which God has set you.

If your hand were severed from your body, your body would live, even though it would be hindered. But your hand, without the life flow of blood from that body, would surely perish. This is why Satan so desires to separate you from the church to which God has called you to be a part. If you become separated from the ministry gifts in your church through which God supplies His anointing, you will be cut off from a primary source of life and nourishment.

What do I mean by "ministry gifts"? I am referring to the offices of ministry listed in Ephesians 4:8,11-13:

> [Jesus] **gave gifts unto men. And he gave some, apostles; and some, prophets; and some, evangelists; and some, pastors and teachers; for the perfecting of the saints, for the work of the ministry, for the edifying of the body of Christ: till we all come in the unity of the faith.**

Notice the progression here. Jesus gives these gifts to the Church so the saints—you and I—will be perfected in order to do the work of the ministry. Incidentally, that word *perfecting* actually means "maturing."

When that happens, the Body of Christ is edified, or built up. This continues **till we all come in the unity of the faith.**

We won't see the full manifestation of this kind of unity until Jesus returns. So until then, these ministry gifts will continue to bring all of us to ever greater levels of spiritual maturity.

Verse 14 reveals our ultimate goal:

> **That we henceforth be no more children, tossed to and fro, and carried about with every wind of doctrine, by the sleight of men, and cunning craftiness, whereby they lie in wait to deceive.**

Just as God has to use people to do His work in the earth, so must Satan, and he has a large number whom he has deceived into unwittingly serving his purpose. There are people Satan uses who lie in wait to deceive you—to try to convince you that something that is untrue and invalid is true and valid, according to our definition.

Of course, because they are deceived, these people don't know that Satan is using them. Still, they just can't wait for an opening to say, "See, I told you this faith stuff doesn't work. God isn't healing today like He did in Bible times. Don't stay in that crazy church. Come back to a church where the people aren't so radical."

You can count on Satan to put someone in your path to say things contrary to whatever promise of God you are standing on in faith. But as you mature in the Word of Truth, you will grow into a place called "the unity of faith." You will be, as it says in Ephesians 4:16, **fitly joined together and compacted.** That is just another way of saying you will be right where you fit the best, are used the most and blessed the greatest.

Mark Them

I want you to see the connection between avoiding deception on one hand and on the other, maturing in the Word of God, coming into the unity of the faith and being fitly joined and compacted with others in the Body of Christ. Maturity is synonymous with unity and knowledge of the truth. Immaturity, on the other hand, means being open to deception and division.

Romans 16:17-18 validates this connection between division and deception:

> Now I beseech you, brethren, *mark them which cause division* and offences contrary to the doctrine which ye have learned; and avoid them. For they that are such serve not our Lord Jesus Christ, but their own belly; and by good words and fair speeches deceive the hearts of the simple.

We are to "mark,"or make note of, those who exhibit a pattern of generating strife and contention in the Body of Christ. Having marked them, we are to avoid them.

It is important to note that these kinds of individuals rarely come across as bad people. They sound good. They are rational and logical, but they use those **good words and**

fair speeches to deceive and cause divisions in the Church. They might even include an old friend, a relative, someone at your workplace or perhaps even a fellow church member. But if their presence in your life starts to pull you from the spot in which God has placed you, then you are to avoid them.

The only right way to do that is first to tell those kinds of people, in love, about the effect they are having on your life. Tell them that what they are doing is scripturally wrong and that you are praying for it to change, but until it does, you just can't open yourself to the divisive influence that is operating through them.

Some people, such as unbelieving family members, probably won't understand. But others who simply may not have known what they were doing will have their eyes opened, and they will make the necessary changes. This is why it is helpful to let divisive individuals know why you are not going to fellowship with them anymore.

I should point out that the word *simple* at the end of Romans 16:18—**They...deceive the hearts of the simple**—is not a reference to those who are less intelligent. This word really means "unsuspecting or naive." The unsuspecting either don't recognize divisive people or don't think that they will be affected. Thus they maintain fellowship with those divisive individuals, often because they think it is the "loving" thing to do.

Don't be naive. You can't mess around with this spirit. It is deadly poison to your spiritual well-being. But you can avoid this deception! You can grow in spiritual maturity and unity with the Body of Christ.

CHAPTER 7

I saw all Israel scattered on the mountains, like sheep which have no shepherd.

I Kings 22:17 NAS

Five Doorways to Division

We have seen the importance of being **fitly joined together and compacted** within the specific church body to which God has called us to be a part. We have seen the lengths to which Satan will go to divide us or isolate us from that church.

Now I want to show you the five divisive influences the Word talks about that, if left to operate unhindered in your life, will open you up to being divided from your vital source of life—your own company of believers.

Number 1: Pastor, Hireling or Wolf?

In John 10, Jesus makes some remarkable statements regarding the importance of a pastor.

Look, for example, at verses 11-14:

> **I am the good shepherd: the good shepherd giveth his life for the sheep. But he that is an hireling, and not the shepherd, whose own the sheep are not, seeth the wolf coming, and leaveth the sheep, and fleeth: and the wolf catcheth them, and scattereth the**

sheep. **The hireling fleeth, because he is an hireling, and careth not for the sheep. I am the good shepherd.**

From the Bible's standpoint, Jesus is the Chief Shepherd, and local pastors are under-shepherds. In fact, the Greek word translated *shepherd* here is also translated "pastor" in most of the other New Testament passages in which it appears.[1]

That tells us some things about the office of pastor. There are three key words in this passage that will enhance your understanding of the truth I am trying to communicate.

The first is the word *wolf.*

Without fail, this word is used in the New Testament to refer to a person who is being used of the devil, sometimes unknowingly, to promote division in the Body of Christ.

Typically, these people love God and don't intend any harm but are spiritual children who haven't grown up in the faith. They simply don't know any better.

The next key word is *scattereth.*

The person acting as a wolf always has the effect of scattering God's flock. The spirit to which the "wolf" has yielded invariably creates division within the local church.

The last key word is *hireling.*

The Lord is telling us that it is possible for a person to stand in the office of pastor who isn't truly called and appointed by God to be there. When that is the case, that pastor will not be able to stop the wolf from scattering the flock.

All too often pastors are hired by a board of deacons or some other committee to do a *job* rather than being appointed and anointed by God to fulfill a calling. Such "hirelings" have no God-given ability to maintain unity or prevent turmoil and schism in their flocks.

When a person truly stands in the office of the pastor, however, he carries an anointing from God to keep the wolf of division away.

Thus the first doorway to division I want to bring to your attention is having a pastor who is not called, appointed and anointed by God. Again, the most basic reason people become isolated from the Body of Christ—and ultimately devoured by Satan—is that they do not have the benefit of the pastoral anointing to supernaturally keep the wolf of division from cutting them off from the Body of Christ.

Why would people allow themselves to be cut off from their church? There are really only three reasons why individuals would be without the covering of the pastoral anointing.

The first is simply neglecting to be committed to a local church. Perhaps they have never heard that God sets every member as it pleases Him, and so they hop around from one meeting to another, not knowing that God has a specific place where He wants them in order to receive their supply.

The second possibility is that they are committed to a church where a hireling stands in the pulpit. How do you determine if the person who is filling the pulpit is called of God? There are two ways: Listen to him preach, and look for the fruit of the ministry. If the anointing is there, you will know it when you hear and see the ministry that comes forth.

The Bible says that sheep know the voice of their shepherd. (John 10:3-27.) When you are in the church to which God has called you, you will recognize the voice coming from that pulpit as God-ordained to speak into your life.

Next, look around the church to see if souls are being saved, people are receiving healing and being filled with the Holy Ghost and are maturing in the things of God.

In other words, judge the tree by its fruit. If there is no good fruit, then the pastor is probably a hireling.

But to get back to our subject, the third reason people might find themselves without the pastoral covering is less apparent. The fact is that the ministry of the pastoral office must be received by faith if one is to benefit from the anointing that flows through it. We are told in 1 Thessalonians 5:12-13 to

Know them which labour among you, and are over you in the Lord, and admonish you; and to esteem them very highly in love for their work's sake.

It is the *office* of ministry you need to esteem highly, not necessarily the *person* who stands in that office. Your faith needs to pull on the anointing that resides in and on the office—not on the talent of the man who stands in it.

Don't be moved by the flaws or failings you may see in the man. Don't fail to hold the office in high esteem simply because the person in it has disappointed you.

All too often people allow the personality of the man to get in the way of the anointing. Perhaps they are irritated by his mannerisms, his accent or something else about his flesh.

You need to look beyond the man to Jesus, who is the author and finisher of your faith.

Every time you sit under your pastor's teaching, believe that God will speak through him into your life and that you will be spiritually fed with exactly what God knows you need. If you will draw on this anointing by faith, you will actually keep the wolf of division out of your life.

Before I leave the subject of the pastoral anointing, I want to show you something else you can draw on from this office.

In Jeremiah 23:4, God shows us what the anointing of the pastor is intended to do;

> **I will set up shepherds over them which shall feed them: and they shall fear no more, nor be dismayed, neither shall they be lacking, saith the Lord.**

As you sit under the ministry of your pastor, you can believe God to feed you exactly what you need to grow up in Christ. Furthermore, you can draw from the office of pastor an anointing that will completely destroy the yoke of fear in your life. Depression can also be a thing of the past. You don't have to get out of bed dreading what the day may hold in store for you.

Your life can be an adventure in God. You can experience no lack of any kind in your life—no lack of love, peace and joy, no lack of health or finances or whatever you need to fulfill God's plan for you.

So if you don't have a God-anointed pastor or you are not rightly relating to the one you have, make the necessary adjustments and close this door of division in your life.

Number 2: Hunger for Supernatural Manifestations

Matthew 7:15 reveals to us the second major doorway
of division:

> **Beware of false prophets, which come to you in
> sheep's clothing, but inwardly they are ravening wolves.**

First of all, the word *prophet* used here simply means
"one who proclaims God's Word." It doesn't necessarily
refer to the office of the prophet but rather more generally
to somebody who proclaims or preaches the Word of God.

Notice that though these people are "ravening wolves"—
people who divide God's flock—they come in sheep's clothing. They don't look like devils. They don't look like bad
people. They look good and sound good, but inwardly they
have a divisive influence on the Body of Christ.

How can you tell if someone is a wolf? Jesus tells us in
the next verse,

> **Ye shall know them by their fruits.**
>
> MATTHEW 7:16

What kind of fruit does a wolf produce? As I have already
said, a wolf scatters and divides the flock. However, in verses
22 and 23 Jesus tells us more about how the wolf operates:

> **Many will say to me in that day, Lord, Lord, have
> we not prophesied in thy name? And in thy name, have
> cast out devils? and in thy name done many wonderful
> works? And then will I profess unto them, I never
> knew you: depart from me, ye that work iniquity.**

"I don't get it, Mac," you might say. "How can prophesy-
ing, casting out devils and doing wonderful works be 'iniquity'?"

They aren't. The iniquity is the division that the wolf brings under the cover of supernatural manifestations.

Please get this. Supernatural manifestations are *not* the measure of a valid ministry. If that is what you primarily hunger for, the devil will surely accommodate you. All too often people go to a meeting somewhere and get "wowed" by all the supernatural manifestations. And when they return to their own church, they suddenly feel frustrated or dissatisfied because they are not seeing those same manifestations in their own services. But by following after manifestations, they can be drawn away from their company by the wolf, become isolated from their designated part of the Body and be vulnerable to attack.

Please don't misunderstand what I am saying. It is good to hunger for more of God's presence and power. As Paul instructs us in 1 Corinthians 12, we should **covet earnestly the best gifts.** But that desire must be built upon a solid foundation.

Jesus tells us how to avoid this kind of deception in Matthew 7:24. He says,

> **Therefore everyone who hears these words of Mine, and acts upon them, may be compared to a wise man, who built his house upon the rock** (NAS).

Jesus is saying, "If you don't want to get drawn off by a ravening wolf with supernatural manifestations, build your search for God's power and presence upon the foundation of My words."

Valid ministry is built only on the Word of God. Supernatural manifestations are awesome, but their purpose is to confirm the Word that is preached. (Mark 16:20.) Your greatest hunger for the things of God must be based on the Word of God first. Then you can flow with the supernatural without the danger of being led astray by manifestations.

Number 3: Itching Ears

In 2 Timothy 4:2, we find the third doorway to division. Here Paul exhorts Timothy to **preach the word, be instant in season, out of season; reprove, rebuke, exhort with all long-suffering and doctrine.**

Very simply, Paul is telling Timothy to preach the whole counsel of God, not just the parts people want to hear. Verse 3 tells us why. *The Amplified Bible* reads this way:

> **For the time is coming when [people] will not toler-ate (endure) sound and wholesome instruction, but, having ears itching [for something pleasant and grati-fying], they will gather to themselves one teacher after another to a considerable number, chosen to satisfy their own liking and to foster the errors they hold.**

This describes a major form of deception, because we all have favorite teachings from God's Word. For some it is the promises concerning healing. For others it is the portions outlining our covenant of increase, provision and prosperity. Still others are drawn to passages concerning the end times.

Whatever promises and passages are your favorites, you must not let your desire for a particular part of the Word, no matter how important it might be to you, bring you to a place of hearing nothing else.

If you are not happy with the Word being preached at the church in which God has set you, then, friend, your ear is beginning to itch! If you scratch it by going someplace where you can hear more of what you *want* to hear instead of the full counsel of God, then you can count on being drawn away, deceived and possibly damaged.

Unfortunately, there are plenty of churches that will tell you that you don't have to tithe, for example. But if you go looking to find a teacher who has a view of Scripture that accommodates your flesh or your biases, you will leave yourself wide open to deception. So don't allow yourself to be drawn away from the place in the Body of Christ in which God has set you.

Number 4: Becoming Offended

Probably the most common way people are separated from the church to which God has called them is by becoming offended at another individual in the church.

Paul, speaking by the Holy Ghost in Acts 24:16, says of this,

Herein do I exercise myself, to have always a conscience void of offense toward God, and toward men.

You see, to have such a conscience is to never allow yourself to feel justified in being offended. You have to be sure you understand just how deadly this tendency is and make a decision not to be offended at anybody, no matter what people say or do.

The reasons people become offended in church are many and varied, but I frequently come across some that are absolutely ridiculous.

"The parking lot attendant wouldn't let me park where I wanted!" said one.

Or how about this—"The music minister just walked right by me without saying a word!"

I've even heard people get offended and say, "I couldn't get an appointment with the pastor as quickly as I wanted!"

Many people get offended because the pastor "steps on their toes" in his preaching. As a pastor myself, I can tell you that your pastor is charged by God to preach the uncompromised Word in such a way as to leave you no "wiggle room" at all—he is not to leave you any way to sneak around the truth.

But if you take that personally instead of receiving it as the operation of the pastoral office, you may get offended at your pastor for not being more sensitive to where you are in your walk with God.

If you become offended at your pastor, then as we have already learned, you are in danger of being cut off from the pastoral anointing that will keep the wolf of division away. Offense allows division and Satan's access into your life.

The tendency to become offended is actually rooted in pride. That is why it is so dangerous. So instead of getting offended, deal with the pride issues that cause offense. And whatever you do, keep this door to division closed.

Number 5: Is It Me?

I need to take you back to a Scripture we have already examined to show you the fifth doorway to division:

> **Now I beseech you, brethren, mark them which**
> **cause divisions and offenses contrary to the doctrine**
> **which ye have learned; and avoid them.**
>
> —ROMANS 16:17

Now, let me be blunt with you for just a moment: Are *you* causing divisions and offenses in your church? Have you allowed yourself, unwittingly, to be used by Satan to divide others from the Body of Christ? If you have, that is bad for those other church members, but it is much worse for you.

Such actions only isolate a person. And as an instrument in the hands of the enemy, a Christian can also encounter a kind of destruction that is hard to even describe. The most miserable, unhappy Christians I know are those who unknowingly fall into that trap of being used by the devil to divide a church.

How can I tell if I am causing division, and what do I do about it? you may be wondering.

The greatest indicator that Satan may try to use you this way is if you tend to be critical. Do you always seem to find fault with everything? Do you tend to see the negative side of things? These are warning signs of a potentially divisive personality.

Basically, people with critical spirits never offer constructive solutions to problems; they just find fault.

The truth is, no one is immune from this disease. We all need to examine ourselves and be watchful. If you are finding it easier to speak negative reports instead of exhorting and promoting the positive, you can ask the Lord to make a change in you. Ask Him to help you see people through His eyes. Ask for the ability to see people with the compassion of Jesus. Ask God to give you ideas that will promote His purpose in the Church. Consciously work to promote unity in the Body.

Of the Same Mind

I want to close by showing you an important passage that speaks on the subject of unity.

> **Now I beseech you, brethren, by the name of our Lord Jesus Christ, that ye all speak the same thing, and that there be no divisions among you; but that ye be perfectly joined together in the same mind and in the same judgment.**
>
> —1 CORINTHIANS 1:10

This is the condition that will release the corporate anointing on a church to change a city for God—unity. After all, if one can put 1000 to flight and two can put 10,000 to flight, what can 10,000 do? (Deut. 32:30.)

When we are all perfectly joined together in the same mind in one accord and without divisions, then the power of God will fall and we will all realize the purpose of God in our lives both corporately and individually. This must be our goal in these last days!

CHAPTER 8

A proud man is always looking down on things and people; and, of course, as long as you're looking down, you can't see something that's above you.

—C.S. Lewis[1]

The Doorway of Pride

Pride is the deadliest enemy of the Christian today.

There is not a Christian alive who doesn't have to deal with the spirit of pride on a daily basis. And if you think pride isn't a problem for you, then perhaps you need to deal with it all the more!

It is a simple truth that our flesh wants to be exalted, recognized and admired. It wants to be looked up to by other people. That is just one of the truths about the clay vessels our spirits inhabit.

Pride has been called the father of all sin, and it is not hard to see why. Lucifer experienced pride. He said, **I will exalt my throne above the stars of God** (Isa. 14:13).

All of the adversity God's creation now experiences began with Lucifer's desire to exalt himself above God. In Ezekiel 28 the Bible tells us that he was lifted up by his own beauty. But his pride brought about the greatest rebellion ever in the kingdom of God, and Lucifer and his fallen angels were expelled from heaven.

Stop and think about this a bit. Why does anybody knowingly disobey God? Isn't it because he thinks he has a better idea?

Pride is the only reason division exists in the Body of Christ. Pride says, *I am right, and I want to have things my way.* Pride is the tendency to exalt *self;* it is the most poisonous evil that a Christian must deal with.

Yes, pride is dangerous. But "religion's" solution to it—self-abasement—is just as bad. Most of the religious world believes that if you flog yourself enough, call yourself a worm and generally walk around acting like you don't deserve to live, that somehow you will have dealt with pride.

The truth is, that kind of self-abasement is really just another form of pride. Abbé de Saint-Cyran once wrote: "There is no greater pride than in seeking to humiliate ourselves beyond measure! And sometimes there is no greater humility than to attempt great works for God."[2]

God says that you are more than a conqueror through Him who loved you. (Rom. 8:37.) He says that you are the righteousness of God in Christ Jesus and that you are able to do all things through Christ who strengthens you. (2 Cor. 5:21; Phil. 4:13.)

But if Satan can't get you into pride, he will try to push you into the opposite "ditch" on the other side of the road—to see yourself as some lowly worm, squashed by the circumstances of life.

How do you stay out of both ditches and walk the right road regarding pride?

Know that pride is self-exaltation but that true humility is not self-abasement. Humility is exalting God through the accomplishments He produces in your life. Recognize that without God you cannot be or do anything but that in Christ there is absolutely nothing you *can't* do.

In Jesus, you are an overcomer. You are a success story looking for a place to happen.

First Corinthians 1:29 gives us an important insight in the matter when it says, **No flesh should glory in his [God's] presence.**

If you want the presence of God in your life, then see to it that He gets the glory for all the good things that He works through you.

If pride is people's biggest challenge, it is also the hardest thing to identify in their lives. It takes courage. After all, who wants to put themselves in the same category as Lucifer?

I want to give you some keys that will help you identify the insidious spirit of pride operating in your life in order to put a stop to it. Before I do though, I need to show you a real-life example of how it can destroy a promising life.

Saul's Example

King Saul was a man used mightily by God; however, through pride, he lost everything—his anointing, his position and eventually, his life. As David said of him in 2 Samuel 1:19, 21:

The beauty of Israel is slain upon thy high places: how are the mighty fallen!...for there the shield of the mighty is vilely cast away, the shield of Saul, as though he had not been anointed with oil.

Saul was completely defeated. But as we have seen, Satan can't defeat us if he can't deceive us, so that means some form of deception preceded Saul's defeat.

As we look at Saul's life, it isn't hard to find the points at which he opened doorways to deception in his life.

Saul opened the door of pride.

Now, Saul wasn't always full of pride. In fact, he started out full of humility. In 1 Samuel 15:17 the prophet addresses Saul:

> **And Samuel said, "Is it not true, though you were little in your own eyes, you were made the head of the tribes of Israel? And the Lord anointed you king over Israel"** (NAS).

Saul started out "little" in his own eyes and thus God could use him. But as soon as he grew in his estimation of himself, his own pride defeated him.

Humility is the only thing that makes any of us useful in the plan and kingdom of God. But if we allow pride to grow in our lives—as it did in Saul's—God's anointing will decrease. And that's the point at which we risk losing the position to which God appointed us.

Lies and Exaggerations

Let's begin our study of the growth of pride in King Saul's life in 1 Samuel 13:

> **And Jonathan smote the garrison of the Philistines that was in Geba, and the Philistines heard of it. And Saul blew the trumpet throughout all the land, saying,**

> Let the Hebrews hear. And all Israel heard say that
> Saul had smitten a garrison of the Philistines.
>
> —1 SAMUEL 13:3,4

Wait a minute, you may be saying to yourself, *It says in
the beginning of verse 3 that* Jonathan *smote the Philistines. But
all Israel heard Saul report that he himself had defeated them.*

This is the first example of Saul's pride I want you to
see: Saul took credit for another man's victory. He was
basically insecure with his own identity and position with
God. As a result, he lied to make himself look better in the
eyes of the people.

We all have to deal with this tendency toward insecurity
from time to time. It may make us want to exaggerate or even
lie about ourselves in order to elevate ourselves in the eyes of
others. It could be a subtle embellishment here or a little inflat-
ing of the details there. But this is one of the ways pride begins
manifesting in your life. You can't treat it lightly—you can't let
this tendency operate in your life, because it will grow.

Watch for it, learn to recognize it and shut the door on it.

Impatience and Arrogance

The second example of Saul's pride is also found in
chapter 13:

> He [Saul] tarried seven days, according to the set
> time that Samuel had appointed: but Samuel came not
> to Gilgal; and the people were scattered from him.
> And Saul said, Bring hither a burnt offering to me,
> and peace offerings. And he offered the burnt offering.
>
> —1 SAMUEL 13:8,9

You can see that Saul arrogantly tried to assume the office and anointing of another man, the prophet. Actually, there are two areas of pride shown here.

The first is impatience, a trap a lot of us fall into when waiting for God's best to unfold. For example, you have probably had at least a glimpse of God's plan for your life. You need to make sure that you don't become impatient while waiting for it to come to pass.

Furthermore, don't "help" God by trying to emulate someone you really respect rather than becoming who God intends *you* to be. Doing so is evidence of attempting to elevate your status ahead of God's timing or to assume an anointing that simply doesn't belong to you.

You need to recognize not only your own gifts and anointing but also those of others. You need to make room for others to operate in their gifts as well. Don't try to usurp someone else's call, responsibility or anointing in an attempt to get things moving more quickly for you, simply because you are unhappy with God's timetable.

Stay with your anointing and calling. Wait on God to promote you. Consecrate yourself not only to God's plan but also to His timing.

A Low Regard for God's Word

We find the next example of Saul's developing pride in Samuel 15. Here the prophet Samuel delivered the Lord's instructions to Saul:

> **Now go and smite Amalek, and utterly destroy all that they have, and spare them not; but slay both**

man and woman, infant and suckling, ox and sheep, camel and ass.

—1 SAMUEL 15:3

I know that looks like a pretty harsh command from God, but it is important to remember that we don't know everything He knows about a given situation. That is why we are told not to lean on our own understanding. (Prov. 3:5.) We must not let humanistic thinking talk us out of the direction God gives us.

We find Saul's response to these instructions in verse 9:

But Saul and the people spared Agag, and the best of the sheep, and of the oxen, and of the fatlings, and the lambs, and all that was good, and would not utterly destroy them: but every thing that was vile and refuse [by their judgment], that they destroyed utterly.

Saul felt free to disregard the command of the Lord for the sake of gaining popularity with the people. This constitutes the third indicator that pride is at work in Saul's life— his lack of reverence for God's command. In other words, he rationalized a way out of doing what God said to do, doing instead what he thought best.

When you do that, you essentially say, "I know what You said, Lord, but I think I have a better idea." If that isn't pride, then I don't know what is!

Blame Shifting

The next indicator of pride is found in verses 20 and 21. Samuel has just confronted Saul with his disobedience:

Saul said unto Samuel, Yea, I have obeyed the voice of the Lord, and have gone the way which the Lord sent me, and have brought Agag the king of Amalek, and have utterly destroyed the Amalekites. But the people took of the spoil.

What Saul did here is called blame shifting, or a failure or refusal to accept responsibility for your actions by pointing to something or somebody else as the reason for your situation.

Of course, blame shifting didn't begin with Saul; it goes all the way back to the Garden of Eden. When God confronted Adam about his disobedience, Adam replied: **The woman whom thou gavest to be with me, she gave me of the tree** (Gen. 3:12).

The next time you get caught in the consequences of your disobedience to God's Word, check yourself to see if you are engaging in self-justification and rationalization instead of taking responsibility. If you are trying to shift the blame, you are walking the same disobedient path that Saul walked.

Sacrifice Instead of Obedience

For the final indicator of pride's growth in Saul's life, we need to return to verses 21 and 22:

The people took of the spoil, sheep and oxen, the chief of the things which should have been utterly destroyed, to sacrifice unto the Lord thy God in Gilgal. And Samuel said, Hath the Lord as great delight in burnt offerings and sacrifices, as in obeying the voice of the Lord? Behold, to obey is better than sacrifice.

—1 Samuel 15:21,22

To obey is better than sacrifice. This isn't the only time the Word of God makes this statement. It is echoed repeatedly throughout Scripture, even by Jesus Himself.

Now, we need to understand this statement and its relevance to us in this dispensation. Sacrifice in the Old Testament was necessary to atone for sin and disobedience. So Samuel is pointing out to Saul, "Sacrifice is good. But since it does make you right with God again, it is better to obey and thus not need to sacrifice."

Today, under the new covenant, Jesus' blood has been shed once and for all. We remove sin from our lives by confessing our sin, according to 1 John 1:9:

> **If we confess our sins, he is faithful and just to forgive us our sins, and to cleanse us from all unrighteousness.**

God *is* faithful and just to forgive you of your sins, but it is better to obey in the first place than to have to confess your sin. Of course, we all miss it from time to time. But if you continually confess the same sin day after day, relying on the provision of confession rather than making a decision to obey God, it may be an indicator of pride working in your life.

You may be using the grace of God as an excuse for sin. (Rom. 6:1.)

Examining One's Self for Pride

As I said at the outset, pride is a deadly thing. That is why it is vital to be able to spot the warning signs of its presence in your life. I would like to quickly review them with you. Ask yourself these questions:

Am I so insecure in my own identity in Christ that I tend to lie and exaggerate to make myself look better?

Do I try to operate in other people's callings or anointing because of impatience or because I think I can stand in someone else's office?

Am I quick to obey God's commands or do I make excuses for doing things my way?

When I experience the consequences of my mistakes, do I shift the blame elsewhere?

Am I continually confessing the same sin over and over again?

If you experience any of these tendencies, then pride may be at work in your life. I believe the Spirit of God is speaking to you now, revealing areas of pride you may not be aware of. Do something about it! Don't let it destroy your life as it did Saul's.

Personal Applications

Has God ever put you in a position in which you felt unqualified or unprepared? Have you ever said, "God, this must be a mistake. You have me in way over my head here"?

There is a reason for that. I have discovered that generally most folks don't have as difficult a time staying humble in an area of life or ministry in which they know they aren't gifted. If God has you doing something for which you have no natural ability or training, you will find it much easier to give Him the glory for what He is doing through you.

God does that on purpose. Take a look at this passage from *The Amplified Bible:*

> **For [simply] consider your own call, brethren; not many [of you were considered to be] wise according to human estimates and standards, not many influential and powerful, not many of high and noble birth. [No] for God selected (deliberately chose) what in the world is foolish to put the wise to shame, and what the world calls weak to put the strong to shame.**
> **—1 CORINTHIANS 1:26,27**

Consider the apostles for a moment. Jesus didn't pick the scholars and learned men of His day. When God needed an ambassador to the Jewish religious establishment, He didn't send Paul, whose resumé would have seemed to make him the perfect candidate for the job. No, He sent Peter—the rough, unlearned fisherman.

Paul, the educated Jewish scholar, was sent to carry the gospel to the "barbarian" Gentiles. God put both men in positions in which they wouldn't be able to lean on their own natural strengths.

Now, I am not trying to say that God won't use your natural ability or education. Of course He will. However, the reason not many wise, influential or powerful people are chosen is that all too often pride causes them to take credit for what they have done instead of giving God the glory for what He did through them.

The point I wish to make is that your greatest vulnerability to pride will be in the area in which you have some expertise or natural talent. You might be good at raising kids. Or maybe you are a skilled organizer or a natural leader.

The trap is thinking that you can accomplish something in your own ability without God. You see, you can begin to lean on your own flesh instead of staying totally dependent on the Lord. When Satan tempts you to receive the glory for a good work, just remember that God said no flesh will glory in His presence. (1 Cor. 1:29.) If you want to keep the presence of God in your endeavors, you must stay humble.

Another area of your life you can examine for evidence of pride is your relationships. How do you treat other people?

Do you know someone who seems to be a constant bother to you? Perhaps this individual is always approaching you with some question or wanting to talk on and on. Do you find yourself thinking, *I can't afford to spend my valuable time with you?*

Let me ask you this: Would you be upset with your boss or pastor if he called you at 2 A.M. to talk? Probably not. Yet God said He is no respecter of persons. (Rom. 2:11.) If you would help your boss in the middle of the night, why not help those others who may not be able to immediately benefit your life?

Friend, if you identify with any of these indications of pride from Saul's life or the other examples we have examined, the poison of pride may be at work in your life. You simply cannot afford to leave it unaddressed; to think otherwise is pure deception.

But we're not going to leave that problem or any other problem with deception unaddressed. Now that we've laid the groundwork for what deception is, we're going to get to the root of how to defeat the deception of pride!

CHAPTER 9

But too many people now climb onto the cross merely to be seen from a greater distance, even if they have to trample somewhat on the one who has been there so long.

—Albert Camus[1]

Dealing With Pride

The Bible does more than help us identify the working of pride in our lives. It also shows us how to eliminate it. I want to share three things from God's Word with you—things you can do to prevent pride from encroaching on your life or to remove it if it is already there.

Lucifer, of course, is our prime example of pride, as we discussed earlier. You would have thought he had everything he could possibly want. In Ezekiel 28:12-15, God says he was **full of wisdom and perfect in beauty.** He was the **anointed cherub that covereth**—meaning God had given him rulership over His creation. God also said of Lucifer: **Thou wast perfect in thy ways from the day thou wast created.**

Yet even with all God had given him, Lucifer came to a place when he said, **I will exalt my throne above the stars of God** (Isa. 14:13). The root of his rebellion was his dissatisfaction with what he had.

He just wanted more.

The fallen Lucifer—now called Satan or the Serpent—then tempted Adam and Eve with the very same thing that caused his fall—pride.

At that time every living thing on this earth was subject to Adam's authority. He was made in the image and likeness of the God who proclaimed that man could partake of every tree in the Garden but one. Yet Adam chose to partake of the only thing that was forbidden to him, because Satan told him it would elevate his status to that of God.

Here is the lesson. If you are acting out of carnal dissatisfaction, then any efforts—even for good things—to promote change in your life will not produce the blessing of God's will, because your motive is to promote yourself.

The antidote to this spirit of dissatisfaction is developing an attitude of contentment.

Develop an Attitude of Contentment

Let's examine what the Bible says about this tendency to be dissatisfied with what we have. Hebrews 13:5 says:

> **Let your conversation** [manner of life] **be without covetousness; and be content with such things as ye have: for he hath said, I will never leave thee, nor forsake thee.**

The Amplified Bible makes this a little clearer. It says,

> **Be satisfied with your present circumstances.**

Now, we can be sure that God is not telling us to be content with any of Satan's work in our lives. That would be contradictory to much of what we find in other parts of the Word. So we are going to need to learn more about what the author of Hebrews means by this phrase.

The best way to do this is to see what else the Word has to say about the subject of contentment. In 1 Timothy 6:6-8, we learn:

> **Godliness with contentment is great gain. For we brought nothing into this world, and it is certain we can carry nothing out. And having food and raiment let us be therewith content.**

If you read the rest of the chapter, you will see that this passage is dealing with the problem of covetousness. For example, verse 10 says, **The love of money is the root of all evil.**

When we get down to verse 17, however, we are told to trust in the living God, **who giveth us richly all things to enjoy.**

God isn't saying that you can never have anything but food and clothing. He is saying that you need to have an attitude of contentment that, when combined with godliness as it says here in verse 6, will produce great gain. *The Amplified Bible* renders that phrase as *immense profit.*

In understanding this, it might help to realize that contentment is a spiritual force just as faith is. Just as fear and faith are opposites, so are dissatisfaction and contentment. The root of dissatisfaction is pride, and if it is left to operate in your life, it will lead you to make decisions that ultimately bring destruction into your life.

Paul sheds a little more light on the subject of contentment in chapter 4 of Philippians when he says:

> **Not that I speak in respect of want: for I have learned, in whatsoever state I am, therewith to be content.**
>
> —PHILIPPIANS 4:11

You can easily see that being content is something you must *learn* to do. Also notice that Paul said he practices contentment *in whatever state.*

You see, you are not to maintain an attitude of contentment just when things are going well. Your spirit of contentment should remain intact through sickness, lack or any other sort of attack. This, however, does not mean you lie back and do nothing about negative circumstances in your life. One chapter earlier Paul declared,

> **I press toward the mark for the prize of the high calling of God in Christ Jesus.**
>
> —PHILIPPIANS 3:14

Once again, *The Amplified Bible* offers additional insight. Philippians 4:11, which we read a moment ago, reads:

> **Not that I am implying that I was in any personal want, for I have learned how to be content (satisfied to the point where I am not disturbed or disquieted) in whatever state I am.**

Here is what the Spirit through the apostle Paul is trying to teach us: No matter what situation you find yourself in, no matter what dire circumstances you face, you are to remain content to the point of not being disturbed or disquieted. If you don't, you actually limit God's ability to lift you out of that situation or those circumstances.

Why is this? Because dissatisfaction comes from thoughts like, *I don't deserve this. Why is this happening to me? I attend church every week and pray every day. I am confessing the right Scriptures. This shouldn't be happening to me.*

Do you see how this is an overly self-concerned attitude? The root of that is pride. Even if you are confessing, praying and believing correctly, God has difficulty in responding because your motive is wrong. When you operate in pride, your desires are self-centered. They basically exalt self. And remember, we learned in 1 Corinthians 1:29, **No flesh should glory in his [God's] presence.**

It is also extremely important that your desire for more of God's presence and power doesn't turn into dissatisfaction with the blessings He has already given you. This is why, in another part of this same chapter in Philippians, Paul encourages us along these lines:

> **Be anxious for nothing, but in everything by prayer and supplication with thanksgiving let your requests be made known to God. And the peace of God, which surpasses all comprehension, shall guard your hearts and your minds in Christ Jesus.**
>
> —PHILIPPIANS 4:6,7 NAS

Pressing Toward the Mark

How do you keep from becoming disturbed or disquieted? First, you do what Paul did. You choose to **press toward the mark for the prize of the high calling of God in Christ Jesus.** If you are making progress toward your divinely appointed destiny in Jesus, you will automatically leave behind the disturbing and disquieting things Satan tries to do in your life.

What is the prize Paul talks about here? Ultimately, of course, it is eternity with God in Heaven. But it also refers to the abundant life in Christ that is available to you now. The Greek word usually translated "life" in the New Testament is *zoe*.[2] It refers to the God-kind of life, the kind of life that Jesus brings when He comes into our lives.

For example, 1 Timothy 6:12 says,

Fight the good fight of faith, lay hold on eternal life [*zoe*], whereunto thou art also called, and hast professed a good profession before many witnesses.

We are to "fight" to "lay hold on" *zoe,* or life with no sickness, no oppression, no lack of any kind.

On Your Mark

In many respects, the concept of pressing toward the mark is the most important of all in Paul's statements here in Philippians 3.

Notice Paul didn't say, "I press toward the prize." Nor did he say that he was pressing toward the high calling. No, it is the mark he has his sights set on. Why?

The mark, as Paul describes it here, is an intermediate goal or objective. If you will focus on it and move toward it, it will keep you on course.

If you know anything about bowling, for example, you know that each lane has on it a series of marks that lie just a few feet in front of the bowler. Good bowlers use these marks to aim their ball so that it ultimately strikes the pins in the proper place. The bowler doesn't aim at the pins—he focuses on the marks.

That is what Paul is talking about here. You may not yet know what your high calling is. The dream God has placed in your heart may not be defined well enough for you to know what to do next. But, praise God, His Word has given us a mark to press toward. Head for that mark, and ultimately God's dream, or *high calling,* for you will come into view.

There is an interesting thing about this mark—it is the same for all of us, no matter how widely our individual callings may vary. It is a universal signpost that will put all who follow it on the winning pathway.

What is this mark we must press toward? In a word, it is *servanthood.*

Jesus established the importance of servanthood with His words and by His example. Remember when the disciples were arguing about who among them was the greatest? Jesus told them the greatest among them was he who would be the servant of all. (Luke 22:24-27.) Later He demonstrated that principle by washing their feet. (John 13:3-15.)

Service is the key to maintaining the *outward* focus that keeps you from becoming disquieted or dissatisfied. It is the mark by which we should measure every decision, every action and every thought.

The problem is, many of us have a negative, stereotypical image of what a servant is. We equate servanthood with slavery and forced servitude. We think that the role of the servant is a degrading one. That is certainly not something we equate with winning.

But if you are going to win the prize of true *zoe* life, you will have to change the way you think about servanthood. You have to realize that it is the winner's way.

When you begin serving with your money—in other words, giving—you will soon find yourself winning in the area of finances. Start serving in the area of relationships—loving—and you will soon reap a winning harvest of love in your own life.

The same principle applies to any and every area of your existence. The more you press toward the mark of service, the more you will find yourself moving into God's marvelous *zoe* life.

Why does that happen? It happens because servanthood releases the very power of God in your life. Isaiah 40:29,31 says it this way:

> **He [God] giveth power to the faint; and to them that have no might he increaseth strength.... They that wait upon the Lord shall renew their strength; they shall mount up with wings as eagles; they shall run, and not be weary; and they shall walk, and not faint.**

The phrase *wait upon* actually refers to a servant's waiting on his master's needs. In other words, as we wait upon God's needs and purposes in the earth, as we serve Him, expecting Him to empower us, He will release the might we need to be winners in every circumstance.

Yes, I said *every circumstance!* Pressing toward the mark of servanthood can turn even the bleakest of situations around 180 degrees.

Job proved that. He had big problems. And no matter how desperate your circumstances are, you probably aren't as bad off as he was. Satan had done his worst in Job's life.

If you read the book of Job, you will see that for some 41 chapters, Job tried to get God to heal him. He was completely focused on his own need the entire time. He clearly loved God, and God clearly loved him. Yet he could not seem to figure out how to get God's divine provision and power operating on his behalf.

Then in chapter 42, Job finally turned his focus outward. He prayed for his friends. He began to serve the needs of others rather than focusing on his own needs, and the power of God was immediately released in his circumstance. Not only was he healed, but he also ended up twice as wealthy as he had been previously.

In your life, just as in Job's, the power of God will be released when you orient your life toward the mark of service to others. It will heal you, restore you and provide for your every need.

In fact, as you press toward the mark of servanthood, the power of God will open doors of opportunity that you never dreamed existed. He will exalt you and give you visibility and influence in your community. He will keep on propelling you toward your dream until one day you will look around and find you have arrived at the high calling of God for your life—the place of fulfillment, the place of meaning and purpose, the place of blessing.

This is how pursuing a godly mark helps you to avoid dissatisfaction. It gives your life meaning and purpose. If you press toward the mark, you press toward a higher place in God. And even though your flesh would rather be somewhere else, you can be satisfied where you are, knowing that if you press the right way, things will change.

You will move ever closer to the prize of the high calling. Additionally, as you gain more of the prize, you will leave more and more of Satan's works behind you.

Let me say one more thing that Paul speaks of in Philippians 3:13, right before he talks about pressing toward the mark. You can't do so until you forget those things that are behind. If you are mindful of past mistakes and failures, you can't give proper attention to pressing forward.

This is especially important to maintaining your contentment, because all dissatisfaction is rooted in the past. If you couldn't remember anything that happened more than one minute ago, you would have nothing to be dissatisfied about. You could only be excited about what tomorrow holds in store for you.

God Will Not Leave You Helpless

Hebrews 13:5 reveals the second point of view you need in order to overcome the temptation to be disturbed and disquieted. Again, *The Amplified Bible* really makes this point clear:

> **Let your character or moral disposition be free from love of money [including greed, avarice, lust, and craving for earthly possessions] and be satisfied with your present [circumstances and with what you have]; for He [God] Himself has said, I will not in any way fail you nor give you up nor leave you**

**without support. [I will] not, [I will] not, [I will] not
in any degree leave you helpless nor forsake nor let
[you] down (relax My hold on you)! [Assuredly not!]**

You can see how emphatic God is here. He will always
meet your need. He will always take care of you if you will
trust Him. When this is a settled issue in your heart, you can
be content in whatsoever state you find yourself. It doesn't
matter what Satan is trying to do in your life; God said He
would not in any way fail you, give you up nor leave you
without support. And don't forget—God said godliness
combined with contentment is a source of immense profit.

You Need Time To Grow

The third thing that will help you to remain satisfied is
found in Luke, chapter 2.

There you can read the account of Jesus' birth and subsequent dedication in the temple when He was eight days old.

From that point on, nothing is revealed about Jesus until
He is twelve years old and Mary and Joseph, after three
frantic days of searching for Him, find Him in the temple.

And after this, nothing more is said of Jesus until He is
thirty years old—except for a small but important detail
about the child Jesus: It says, **He increased in wisdom and
stature, and in favour with God and man** (Luke 2:52).

In other words, He grew in the things of God.

Now, if Jesus Himself needed to grow up in the things of
God, then surely we do too. Many of the things we get so
impatient about are simply a matter of growing in God.
Many of the "due seasons" that must pass in our lives before

we receive from God are directly related to becoming mature enough to handle the thing God wants to give us.

God simply won't give you a huge amount of responsibility that you can't manage. Growth takes time, and just as in Jesus' life, there will be some silent years in yours. Don't become dissatisfied with where you are; just let God continue to prepare you for the next level by pressing toward the mark that He sets before you.

If you find yourself becoming impatient and thinking, *I don't want to wait anymore. I want to do what God has shown me now!* it is a sign that pride is manifesting in you, and you will need to deal with it.

Be patient. It takes time to grow in God. While you grow, keep in mind that God will never leave you nor let you down. Forget what is behind, and keep pressing toward the mark He sets before you. God will see you through your present situation.

You *can* overcome the temptation to be disturbed or disquieted. You *can* become a person who remains content. And as such a person, you will be in line for increase in the kingdom of God.

Thus the first step to closing the door to pride is to eliminate dissatisfaction and become a person of contentment.

Develop A Heart of Gratitude

The second major thing you can do to drive pride out of your life is stated in Romans 1:21-22:

When they knew God, they glorified him not as God, neither were thankful; but became vain in their

imaginations, and their foolish heart was darkened. Professing themselves to be wise, they became fools.

It is important that you see the progression in this Scripture. First, they knew God but didn't give Him glory. Second, they were not thankful and became vain, or empty, in their imaginations. Third, their hearts were darkened, or deceived, and they were in pride by professing themselves to be wise.

The simple truth of this verse is that you ultimately will become *prideful* if you do not learn to be *thankful*. Fortunately, becoming a thankful person involves nothing more than making a quality decision to have a heart of thanksgiving, to look on the light side of every situation instead of the dark side. It is a decision to focus your attention on what God has already blessed you with instead of what you don't have.

If you don't know how to be thankful, you will likely make the wrong decision by default, because you can always count on Satan to bring the negative to your attention. He will be sure to remind you of your needs and wants instead of what you've already been blessed with.

Always focusing on the negative will keep you from being thankful and eventually will lead to your becoming bitter and resentful. The root of all this is pride—and that pride is based on the assumption that you deserve better.

What you are really doing is implying that God is not just. (It helps to remember that if we all got what we deserved, we would all be burning in hell right now!)

Start looking daily for a blessing for which you can be thankful. Do this the most when you feel like doing it the least. Resist the temptation to call other people's attention to your situation in order to garner a little pity from them. Just refuse to look on the dark side, and instead find something you can thank God for.

Build upon your foundation of contentment a house of thanksgiving to God for all His blessings in your life. Become someone who has a heart of gratitude, and you will close a major door to pride and deception in your life.

True Humility

The focus of this entire chapter has been on how to close the door to the deception of pride—the mother of all sins. Nothing slams that door as completely as pride's opposite—humility.

If you can learn to truly humble yourself, pride won't stand a chance.

Let me say this again: True Bible humility is a recognition that without God you are nothing but that with God, you can do absolutely anything—and give Him all the glory for it.

Biblical humility eliminates the "me, myself and I" orientation in your life. In other words, it removes selfishness as a motivation for the things you do. Selfishness is really, in this context, almost a synonym for pride, in that dealing with pride requires you to remove *self* as a motivation for what you do.

This is called dying to self. It is a putting to death of the tendency of your flesh to motivate you to serve your own interests. This is what constitutes genuine Bible humility.

Once you have taken self out of the picture, you can really be excited about where your life is going, because then it is God who is orchestrating your life rather than you.

Just how important is humility? We get a feel for its value in 1 Peter 5:5-6:

> **Likewise, ye younger, submit yourselves unto the elder. Yea, all of you be subject one to another, and be clothed with humility: for God resisteth the proud, and giveth grace to the humble. Humble yourselves therefore under the mighty hand of God, that He may exalt you in due time.**

Pride doesn't just open the door to Satan; it causes God Himself to resist you. That is not a place in which you want to find yourself.

The wonderful truth about humility is that it is the key to walking in God's increase and blessings. If you humble yourself (*you* have to do this; don't ask God to do it for you) under God's mighty hand, you enable Him to exalt you, lift you up and honor you before men. Then when you are in this exalted position, you give God the glory instead of taking the credit yourself. God's kingdom receives greater visibility and increase as a result of your light shining in the darkness of this world.

We all love to read the part about God's exalting us. But don't skip over the "in due time" part. That means don't get impatient. Remember, impatience says, *My time is too valuable to be in this condition or place any longer.* That kind of pride is an indicator that your due season needs to run a little longer.

Your due season is approaching its end when it doesn't matter to you anymore. You are content. You aren't disturbed or disquieted. You are thankful for God's blessings. You know that God will exalt you in time, and you don't want it before then because you know you couldn't handle it anyway.

So how do you stop being self-centered? How do you come to a place of humility, when your motive is no longer to serve your own self-interest but rather to exalt and magnify God and His kingdom?

Jesus, of course, is our primary example of humility, so let's get some insights into His life from Philippians 2:

> **If there be therefore any consolation in Christ, if any comfort of love, if any fellowship of the Spirit, if any bowels and mercies, fulfil ye my joy, that ye *be likeminded,* having the same love, being of one accord, of *one mind....* But in *lowliness of mind* let each esteem other better than themselves.**
>
> **—PHILIPPIANS 2:1-3**

What is on your mind today? Serving *your* needs and interests or serving someone else's? We get more insight into what this mind-set looks like in the subsequent verses.

> **Look not every man on *his own things,* but every man also on *the things of others.***
>
> **—PHILIPPIANS 2:4**

A similar question is, Whose stuff is on your mind?

> **Let this mind be in you, which was also in Christ Jesus.**
>
> **—PHILIPPIANS 2:5**

What mind did Jesus have?

Who, being in the form of God, thought it not robbery to be equal with God: but made himself of no reputation, and took upon him the form of a servant, and was made in the likeness of men: and being found in fashion as a man, he humbled himself, and became obedient unto death, even the death of the cross. Wherefore God also hath highly exalted him, and given him a name which is above every name.

—PHILIPPIANS 2:6-9

The progression in verses 8 and 9 is extremely important: He humbled himself and became obedient, and then God exalted Him.

Humility produces obedience. When you are obedient to the Word to the point that you die to self, God can highly exalt you as He did Jesus.

Let me say this to you: You will never be consistently obedient to the Word of God until you humble yourself. A stronghold of pride in your life can make you think you know what is best for you even though the Bible says otherwise. You may make excuses for why you just can't do what the Word says right now.

What produces humility? Having the mind of a servant.

Earlier we examined the need to press toward the mark of service. There is a lot more that can and should be said on this life-changing subject.

In fact, servanthood is the third way to close the doorway to pride in your life. It is also where real contentment lies. Start serving someone else's needs, and one day you will discover that you are happier than you have ever been.

The spirit of self-pity will be long gone. I want you to see this as a principle that will put you on the road to God's high calling for your life. In Mark 10:43-45 Jesus put it this way:

Whosoever will be great among you, shall be your minister: and whosoever of you will be the chiefest, shall be servant of all. For even the Son of man came not to be ministered unto, but to minister, and to give His life a ransom for many.

God promotes servants into positions of authority. You can subordinate your flesh, humble yourself, remove selfishness from your life and allow God to exalt you—all through serving other people.

The natural question to ask at this point is, "How do I serve?"

Again, Jesus is our example. Everything Jesus did on this earth was for the purpose of revealing the Father's heart to a lost and dying world. Bringing people to Him is precisely how we are to serve other people in this life. That's the only way we can serve anybody in a meaningful fashion. That means serving them His Word using every resource we have available.

Certainly there are things you can and should do as an individual to serve. However, the most basic and most effective way to serve is to make your resources available to the part of the Body of Christ to which God has called you—your local church. God designed the local church to reach the lost and help believers grow into the image of Jesus. The church enables your supply of time, finances and prayer to produce the most fruit for the kingdom of God.

Another way to serve is in your family. Serving in your church may be the most effective way of reaching large numbers of people for Christ, but serving your family will reveal more about your understanding of this principle.

Serving those who are closest to you and who know you the best can be more difficult because you are with them a lot more than anybody else is.

Do you see yourself as a servant to your spouse? Your children? Your parents? And to those of you who are employers or managers, do you see yourself as a servant to those who work for you? You see, the more authority you have, the more you are required to serve those who are accountable to you.

Washing Feet

There is something very powerful I want you to see in John 13:4-8.

> He [Jesus] riseth from supper, and laid aside his garments; and took a towel, and girded himself. After that he poureth water into a basin, and began to wash the disciples' feet, and to wipe them with the towel wherewith he was girded. Then cometh he to Simon Peter: and Peter saith unto him, Lord, dost thou wash my feet? Jesus answered and said unto him, What I do thou knoweth not now; but thou shalt know hereafter. Peter saith unto him, Thou

shalt never wash my feet. Jesus answered him, *If I* *wash thee not, thou hast no part with me.*

If you refuse to serve those who serve you, you have no part with Jesus. If you don't serve others, how will you ever close the door to pride? And if you don't close that door, then as a result, you will always be open to Satan's deceptions.

Jesus went on to say in verses 15-17:

I have given you an example, that ye should do as I have done to you. Verily, verily, I say unto you, The servant is not greater than his lord; neither he that is sent greater than he that sent him. If ye know these things, happy are ye if ye do them.

If Jesus can wash the feet of His disciples, then surely you can wash the feet of your spouse or your children. You can even wash the feet of someone you dislike!

Do it by faith and say, "Lord, I want to be able to serve from my heart. I want the very last remaining bit of pride removed from my life." You will see a miracle happen as the yoke of pride is supernaturally broken off of your life.

Don't allow the "demon" of self to rule you any longer. To close the door to pride once and for all, deal with discontent, become a thankful person and purpose in your heart to be a servant to others.

CHAPTER 10

Wealth is like a viper, which is harmless if a man knows how to take hold of it; but if he does not, it will twine round his hand and bite him.

—St. Clement[1]

The Deceitfulness of Riches

In chapter 4 of Mark we find one of the best-known parables in the Bible—the parable of the sower. I actually think a more accurate title would be "The Parable of the Soils," because in it Jesus describes four possible conditions of the human heart in terms of its receptivity to the seed of God's Word.

Right in the middle of Jesus' interpretation of this parable, we discover the next doorway to deception:

> **And the cares of this world, and *the deceitfulness of riches,* and the lusts of other things entering in, choke the word, and it becometh unfruitful.**
>
> **—MARK 4:19**

All too many times the phrase *the deceitfulness of riches* is interpreted to mean "riches are deceitful," and so it has been widely taught that we should avoid riches.

Now, there *is* a clear warning for us in this verse, to be sure. Jesus warns us that the very prosperity God desires for us can open us to the potential for deception. As it says in Proverbs, **The prosperity of fools shall destroy them** (Prov. 1:32).

But this is a gross misunderstanding of the truth Jesus is presenting here. Throughout the Word, we see that God wants us to experience abundance. He even **delights in the prosperity of His servants** (Ps. 35:27 NAS).

In fact, you can't be effective at what God has called you to do unless you prosper and increase in the kingdom of God.

So the key to not being destroyed by prosperity is to not be a fool!

It is vital that you understand how the deception of "riches" might manifest. If you are forewarned, then Satan can't draw you down that path. So I want to show you three different ways Satan tries to deceive people with money, depending on their economic condition.

The Desire To Be Rich

The first deception I will deal with tends to work on those who don't have enough or who perhaps are barely making ends meet.

First Timothy 6:9-10 describes this deception:

> **Those who desire [crave] to be rich fall into temptation and a snare, and into many foolish and harmful lusts which drown men in destruction and perdition.** *For the love of money is a root of all kinds of evil,* **for which some have strayed from the faith in their greediness, and pierced themselves through with many sorrows** (NKJV).

The word *love* is the operative term in this passage. It is translated from the Greek word *agape,* which I would paraphrase to mean "a love that prompts you to give of yourself."[2]

So in other words, this passage means that to give yourself to the pursuit of money or the things money can buy opens you to every form of evil.

Once that happens, you have strayed from the faith, or become deceived, and you will ultimately "pierce yourself through with many sorrows."

You might be thinking at this point, *How do you know this is just talking about the poor? This sounds like it could apply to almost anyone.*

I know it is about the poor because of the context of the passage. The previous verse (v. 8 NKJV) dealt with having food and clothing but nothing more. It speaks of having nothing but the bare essentials.

Then the passage goes on to talk about "those who desire to be rich."

These people obviously aren't rich *yet.*

The potential deception is in developing a hunger for money in the belief that if you just had enough of it, you would be happy, fulfilled and content. What drives a hunger for money and deceives people into pursuing what money can buy is the belief that more money will bring relief from their present circumstances.

This is a lie from Satan. He wants you to think that everything would be all right if you just had a little more money.

Money is morally neutral. It is neither good nor evil. The Bible merely says that *the love of* money is a root of all evil, not money itself.

You see, you need money to help you fulfill the call of God on your life. However, money is never to be the motivation behind what you do. Don't let the pursuit of money be the foundation for the decisions you make.

The financial prosperity that is clearly God's will for your life carries with it the potential to rob you of your hunger for God. If you are hungry for money and what it can buy in this natural realm, then you will lose your appetite for God and the spiritual realm. So the Word tells you to be forewarned.

How do you stay out of this deception? Paul tells us in 1 Timothy 6:8:

Having food and raiment let us be therewith content.

And again, in Philippians 4:11 Paul writes:

I have learned, in whatsoever state I am, therewith to be content.

Of course, as we discussed in the previous chapter, Bible contentment is avoiding becoming disturbed or disquieted about your present circumstances. If you combine that with godliness, as Paul says in 1 Timothy 6:6, you have a source of "great gain," or as *The Amplified Bible* says, "immense profit."

If you will live a godly life, base your life on obedience to the Word and be content, God can lift you out of the place of financial insufficiency.

Let me summarize this by saying that faith is *rest*. If you are truly in faith, God will bring increase to your life because it is His promise to you. And then you can rest where you are and be undisturbed, satisfied and content, knowing that where you're at now is just temporary.

Contentment is an indicator that you are in faith. Conversely, if you are not content, then you may not be in faith.

"The Power of My Hand"

The second kind of deception associated with riches comes into play as you begin to prosper. As increase begins in your life, you must be on guard against being satisfied by riches instead of by God.

We find a relevant warning about the deception that can come with having riches in Deuteronomy. It begins with a description of increasing prosperity:

Therefore thou shalt keep the commandments of the Lord thy God, to walk in His ways, and to fear [reverence] him.

For the Lord thy God bringeth thee into a good land, a land of brooks of water, of fountains and depths that spring out of valleys and hills; a land of wheat, and barley, and vines, and fig trees, and pomegranates; a land of oil olive, and honey; a land wherein thou shalt eat bread without scarceness, thou shalt not lack any thing in it; a land whose stones are iron, and out of whose hills thou mayest dig brass.

When thou hast eaten and art full, then thou shalt bless the Lord thy God for the good land which he hath given thee.

—DEUTERONOMY 8:6-10

I want you to notice God said, **When thou hast eaten and art full....** God did not say *if*, because when you act on God's Word, you *will* be full and satisfied. But when that happens, you need to heed the warning that follows, beginning in verse 11:

> **Beware that thou forget not the Lord thy God,** in not keeping his commandments, and his judgements, and his statutes, which I command thee this day: lest when [again, not *if*] thou hast eaten and art full, and hast built goodly houses [that's right, more than one], and dwelt therein; and when thy herds and thy flocks multiply, and thy silver and thy gold is multiplied, and all that thou hast is multiplied; *then thine heart be lifted up, and thou forget the Lord thy God....*
>
> —DEUTERONOMY 8:11-14

Don't ever let anyone tell you that God doesn't want you wealthy. If He didn't want you to have wealth, then He wouldn't have given you the power to acquire it:

> **But thou shalt remember the Lord thy God: for it is he that giveth thee power to get wealth, that he may establish his covenant which he sware unto thy fathers, as it is this day.**
>
> —DEUTERONOMY 8:18

Every ability, talent, skill and spiritual gift you possess was given to you by God to enable you to "establish His covenant." This verse makes it clear that getting wealth is instrumental in doing that.

God wants you to increase in order to establish His covenant in the earth, not to satisfy your own cravings. It takes money to preach the gospel to the world, to tell people about Jesus and get them saved. To that end, God has given you the power to get wealth.

You need to keep this in mind, because our natural tendency is to take credit for the increase that comes. You fall into this deception when you begin to think, *Look at how well I'm doing. Look how successful I have become. Look at this awesome deal I put together. My power and the might of my hand have gotten me this wealth.*

When you have thoughts of that nature, it means you are forgetting that God is your source. The "deceitfulness of riches" is effecting your heart.

The good news is, God has given us a powerful and effective way to remind ourselves of His ownership and our stewardship over the riches He brings to us. Simply tossing up a "Thank You, Lord" every now and then isn't enough. There is a scriptural way we are to remember, and it is the preventative medicine for this kind of deception.

You see it in Deuteronomy 26:1-2:

> **And it shall be, when thou art come in unto the land which the Lord thy God giveth thee for an inheritance, and possessest it, and dwellest therein; that thou shalt take of the first of all the fruit of the earth...and shalt go unto the place which the Lord thy God shall choose to place His name there.**

God is telling you to take your firstfruits—or in other words, your tithe—to the local church to which He has assigned you. The tithe is to be your supernatural point of remembrance of all that God has done in your life so you don't begin to take credit for the increase that comes.

Look what God commands you to do in verses 10 and 11 of that same chapter. The tither is instructed to declare:

> **Now, behold, I have brought the firstfruits of the land, which thou, O Lord, hast given me. And thou shalt set it before the Lord thy God, and worship before the Lord thy God: and thou shalt rejoice in every good thing which the Lord thy God hath given unto thee, and unto thine house.**

Don't just drop your tithe in the bucket. Make it a touch-point of remembrance and say, "God, I thank You for all the good things You did for me last week, last month and last year. I praise You for the faithfulness You have demonstrated in my life."

Make your tithe a consistent, personal reminder that God, not your own cleverness or strength, is the source of your blessings.

Do this and you will close the door to this form of deception.

Trusting in Uncertain Riches

To discover the third way Satan deceives people with money, we need to go back to 1 Timothy 6:17:

> **Charge them that are rich in this world, that they be not high-minded, nor trust in uncertain riches, but in the living God, who giveth us richly all things to enjoy.**

Just as riches present one type of deceitfulness to the person who is struggling financially and a different type to the person who is experiencing increase, there is another type of trap for those who are already rich.

The first thing you need to be watchful for if you fall into this category is, when you become successful, arrogance and pride creeping in your life.

Before you conclude that this doesn't apply to you because you don't consider yourself rich, let me define the word *rich* in this verse. In the Greek, it simply means "having an excess beyond need," with no particular amount of excess specified.[3] Whether it is a million dollars or one dollar, if you have discretionary income—which is anything beyond your need—the Bible defines you as rich.

The deception you need to resist when you are rich in this world is trusting in money rather than in God. But people don't like to admit they have begun trusting in money more than their heavenly Father. That is why this deception is so easy to slip into.

When you are financially well off, it can be easier to just go buy what you need rather than trust God for it. But when you have to use your faith for your next meal, it is in a sense easier to stay focused on Him.

Beware of the tendency to stop trusting God to meet your needs when you have excess. The attitude, *Why trust God when I have the money to make it happen on my own?* is a dangerous deception.

Jesus demonstrated this truth so clearly in His dealing with the rich young ruler we find in Matthew 19.

This young man came to Jesus, asking, **Good Master, what good thing shall I do, that I may have eternal life?**

Jesus replied, **Keep the commandments.**

The young ruler said, **All these things have I kept from my youth up: what lack I yet?**

Jesus answered, **Go and sell [all] that thou hast, and give to the poor.** (vv. 16-21.)

At that, the young man walked away sadly because he had great possessions. Faced with the decision to trust in Jesus or his wealth, he turned and walked away from eternal life and *heavenly* riches beyond imagination.

That is when Jesus made this often misunderstood statement:

It is easier for a camel to go through the eye of a needle, than for a rich man to enter into the kingdom of God.

—MATTHEW 19:24

Understand that Jesus is not saying that you cannot go to Heaven if you are rich.

Let's give this statement some cultural perspective. You see, the walls surrounding cities of that day were made up of several big gates and one smaller gate designed for pedestrians. The smaller gate was known as "the eye of the needle."

Now, if people wanted to lead their camels through the eye of the needle, it was possible—but only if they unloaded the camel and got it down on its knees. It was possible, but difficult.

Jesus was using this metaphor to make the point that if you are a rich person it may be harder for you to walk in the things of God and inherit the kingdom. Not impossible, just more difficult.

"How can I tell if I am trusting in money instead of God?" you may ask.

Take the same test Jesus gave the rich young ruler. Ask yourself, *If God asked me to sell everything and give it all to Him, could I do it?*

If you couldn't, then there is a door open to this brand of deception in your life.

Now, don't you dare misquote me on this. I am not saying that giving everything you have to God is a requirement for following Him. There are many rich people in the Bible, such as Abraham, King David and King Solomon to name just a few. And they were men who served God with glorious distinction without having to sell all to follow Him. God could use them because they were willing to use their resources for God's purpose.

King David beautifully expressed his heart to give in 1 Chronicles 29:14:

Who am I...[to] be able to offer thus so willingly? For all things come from You, and out of Your own [hand] we have given You (AMP).

So how can you defend yourself against the powerful temptation to trust in your riches rather than God? First Timothy 6:18 tells us that *giving* is the key:

Instruct them to do good, to be rich in good works, to be generous and ready to share (NAS).

The remedy for being high-minded and placing your trust in uncertain riches is to be generous to the point of giving all if necessary. Just realize that God doesn't measure generosity by the amount you give but rather by the percentage you give. Jesus said the poor widow with the two mites gave more than the rest because she gave all that she had. (Matt. 12:41-44.)

You may not have much to give right now, but that is all right. Just be generous with what you do have.

Working for a "Giving"

As I close this chapter, I want to make one more comment. It is difficult to avoid these deceptions concerning money if you view the purpose of work in the same way the fallen world does—in other words just "working for a living."

Paul gives us the biblical perspective concerning work and career:

> **Let him that stole steal no more: but rather let him labour, working with his hands the thing which is good, that he may have to give to him that needeth.**
>
> —EPHESIANS 4:28

According to this perspective, you are not working for a *living;* you are working for a *giving.* You are not to labor merely so you can retire early, buy a big house on the lake and lie around in a hammock. And in fact, God isn't necessarily against those things. In fact, He wants you to have them. But your motive for working is *not* to be the acquisition of things.

Your greatest happiness, your greatest blessings and your greatest fulfillment will come when you do what you do with the intent to be a blessing to others. You are to labor in this life so that, after you pay your tithe and meet your family's needs, you will have something left over that God can use to meet someone else's need.

Since mankind's most basic need is to be reconciled to God, the main focus of your life's effort needs to be to get Jesus preached to the unsaved and the Word of God to other believers so they can mature in it.

When you have this mind-set—that all of your resources belong to God and you will do with them as He directs you—then Satan will no longer be able to deceive you with riches.

CHAPTER 11

A man who walks by day will not stumble, for he sees by this world's light. It is when he walks by night that he stumbles, for he has no light.

John 11:9,10 NIV

Deception That Produces Illness

Before I begin discussing the deception that produces illness, I want to share one thing: The last thing in the world I would ever want to do is hurt your feelings. My purpose is not to offend you or make you uncomfortable. But I owe you the truth. In this important chapter I am going to make some statements—statements that I'm convinced are consistent with the Word of God—that some Christians simply don't want to hear.

That is why I am hoping you will open your heart to the Spirit of God and stay with me to the end. If you will, I believe that you will learn things that will change your life.

I believe that you are about to learn some keys that can help you walk in the supernatural health Jesus died to purchase for you.

So just stay open and sensitive to the Spirit of God!

What I want to show you is this. The persistent presence of sickness, disease or infirmity of any sort in a person's body may be a sign that there is an area of deception somewhere in that person's heart. Now, remember that *deception*, by definition, is believing that something is true or valid when it is actually untrue or invalid.

How can I say that so boldly? I have scores of scriptural reasons.

In the beginning of this book, I said that there is very little the devil can do in the life of a believer without first *deceiving* him in some area.

This truth extends to every aspect of redemption. And as I am about to show you, health and healing are clearly part of the redemptive work Jesus suffered and died to accomplish.

For example, look at Isaiah 53:4-5. It is the passage which prophesies Jesus' crucifixion in great detail and explains what it would bring about in terms of the redemption.

> **Surely** [not *maybe]* **he hath borne our griefs** [literally *pains*]**, and carried our sorrows** [literally *sicknesses]*: **yet we did esteem him stricken, smitten of God, and afflicted. But he was wounded for our transgressions, he was bruised for our iniquities: the chastisement of our peace was upon him;** *and with his stripes we are healed.*

This is an unequivocal declaration from the Word of God. Period. Case closed. Discussion over.

Should there be any doubt remaining about whether this part of Jesus' redemptive work carried over into the new covenant, a quick reading of 1 Peter 2:23-24 would remove it:

> **Who, when he [Jesus] was reviled, reviled not again; when he suffered, he threatened not; but committed himself to him that judgeth righteously:**

who his own self bare our sins in his own body on the tree, that we, being dead to sins, should live unto righteousness: *by whose stripes ye were healed.*

Peter quoted the passage in Isaiah and applied it directly to his Christian readers! The only thing he did was change one word: Peter quoted it in the past tense—**were healed**—signifying that in Christ our healing is a completed reality!

You are not "the sick" *trying* to get healed. You are "the healed," and Satan is trying to steal your health with the only weapon he has—deception. Of course, some try to explain 1 Peter 2:24 away by claiming that it applies only to "spiritual" healing.

Before you buy into that theory, you had better take a look at Matthew 8:16-17:

When the even was come, they brought unto him many that were possessed with devils: and he cast out the spirits with his word, and healed all that were sick: that it might be fulfilled which was spoken by Esaias [Isaiah] the prophet, saying, Himself took our infirmities, and bare our sicknesses.

Here we have yet another New Testament Scripture telling us how to interpret Isaiah 53. The Word of God is telling us here that Jesus ministered healing to the sick in fulfillment of Isaiah's prophecy. Certainly this includes soulish, emotional and spiritual healing but, make no mistake about it, you have also been redeemed from physical sickness by what Jesus did on the Cross.

By the stripes of Jesus, you *were* and *are* healed.

Remember now, the primary weapon Satan has is deception. So in order for you to be sick, you must first be deceived. You have to start believing something other than God's Word before sickness can actually occur in your body.

Be aware that any kind of deception left to operate in your life can result in sickness. But I would like to highlight the forms of deception that most frequently hinder your ability to walk in the healing Jesus died to provide for you.

The Source of Sickness

One issue which Satan uses to deceive many Christians centers on the origin, or source, of sickness.

Jesus didn't have any confusion on the issue. In John 10:10 the Lord makes a clear declaration on the matter:

> **The thief cometh not, but for to steal, and to kill, and to destroy: I am come that they might have life, and that they might have it more abundantly.**

The devil is the one in the killing and destroying business. Jesus, on the other hand, is in the life-giving business. More than once He made it clear that He was sent to undo the devil's handiwork. And a Scripture in Acts confirms that sickness and disease are works of the enemy:

> **How God anointed Jesus of Nazareth with the Holy Ghost and with power: who went about doing good, and *healing all that were oppressed of the devil;* for God was with him.**
>
> —ACTS 10:38

Here Luke makes it clear that being sick is equivalent to being oppressed of the devil.

Nevertheless, countless believers wring their hands in doubt and uncertainty, thinking that perhaps their illness has come from God as a test of some sort. They do so in spite of the fact that in James we are forbidden to even suggest such a thing!

> **Let no man say when he is tempted** [tried or undergoing tribulation], **I am tempted of God: for God cannot be tempted with evil, neither tempteth he any man.... Do not err, my beloved brethren. Every good gift and every perfect gift is from above, and cometh down from the Father of lights, with whom is no variableness, neither shadow of turning.**
> —JAMES 1:13,16

Is cancer, for example, a good and perfect gift? Let no one say so! God tests no one with the works of the devil. Of course, God may test your obedience from time to time, but He would never use as a tool something from which His precious Son suffered and died to redeem you.

Read the Gospels, and see if you can show me one instance in which Jesus encountered a well person and proceeded to put sickness upon him in order to teach him a lesson. Show me one occasion when Jesus took the life of some mother's son in order to make her a stronger person or equip her for a ministry to other grieving mothers. No! Jesus broke up every funeral He ever encountered and healed every sick person he could.

Sickness and death came into our lives at the Fall. Jesus came to restore what was lost, and we must not ever—even for a moment—allow the enemy to confuse us about the source of sickness. It is a deception that will utterly drain you of the power to overcome it.

God's Will To Heal

The first thing that must be firmly established in your heart if you are to successfully stand against sickness is that it *is* the will of God to heal. If you are not convinced, you are going to have a hard time receiving your healing by faith.

Romans chapter 4 tells us that Abraham appropriated God's promise by being **fully persuaded** of its truth and of God's faithfulness to bring it to pass.

> **He staggered not at the promise of God through unbelief; but was strong in faith, giving glory to God; and being fully persuaded that, what he had promised, he was able also to perform.**
>
> —ROMANS 4:20,21

Like Abraham, we must be fully persuaded where God's promises of health and healing are concerned.

More than anything, Satan wants you to question God's Word. It was his strategy with Eve in the Garden, and it is his strategy against you. So rest assured that he will send people across your path who say that they have tried "that faith and healing stuff" and it didn't work for them. He will even have you introduced to relatives of Christians who died while believing for their healing.

But God says we are not to be moved by natural circumstances or by what we see. We walk by faith, not by sight, according to 2 Corinthians 5:7. We are to be moved only by the Word of God.

We should never hold up people's experiences—or even our own—against the integrity of God's Word.

Nevertheless, many people decide that it must not always be God's will to heal because of something tragic that happened to somebody else. The trouble with this reasoning is that no one but God knows another person's heart.

No one can know whether there was fear, unforgiveness or perhaps some area of disobedience in the life of the person who has died. In fact, there may be some secret issue of the heart that hindered the manifestation of healing. Truly God and God alone knows what door to deception was left open in that person's life that allowed destruction to occur.

Of course, there is always a theologian somewhere who will try to convince you that God put sickness on you to punish you for your disobedience or that God is using sickness to "teach you something."

The Bible is very clear about how God teaches His children. He teaches them through His Word and by the Holy Spirit. (John 14:26; 16:13; 2 Tim. 3:16; 1 John 2:27 and so forth.)

You cannot base your belief on another person's opinion (including mine). You have to examine for yourself what the Word of God says. You have eyes. You can read. You have a brain and a spirit. You can understand and perceive the truth in the Word. What does it say?

Again, it says that Jesus came that we might have life and have it more abundantly. It says that with his stripes we were healed.

Settle this issue in your heart once and for all. No matter what circumstance, symptom, testimony or doctor's report Satan brings against you, do not allow him to move you off your stand on the truth of God's Word.

An Unbiblical Lifestyle

Some people are battling sickness in their bodies simply because they don't give any consideration to how they live.

You don't need to wonder why your healing hasn't manifested if you are disregarding things in your life the Lord has dealt with you about. It could be something as seemingly innocuous as listening to secular music, watching R-rated movies or keeping up with soap operas. But the fact is, if you are consuming those things, then you are feeding yourself darkness from this world's system. You are literally feeding yourself death.

If a person is consistently and willfully being disobedient to God's Word, continuing to do things that he knows the Bible says are wrong, he has moved himself out from under the protecting power of the blood of Jesus. He has inadvertently given Satan access to his life.

King Hezekiah is a good example of this. In Isaiah 38, we learn that Hezekiah was sick unto death.

Now, Hezekiah had previously entered into a covenant with Egypt against the Assyrians in direct violation of God's Word.

Isaiah came to him and said, **Thus saith the Lord, Set thine house in order: for thou shalt die, and not live.**

Hezekiah then **turned his face toward the wall, and prayed unto the Lord.**

That is an Old Testament way of saying that he repented. God then sent Isaiah back to Hezekiah to tell him, **Behold, I will add unto thy days fifteen years.**

Like Hezekiah, many people are sick in their bodies because they fail to deal with sin, not realizing its effect on their lives. If you allow disobedience to continue, you open yourself up to sickness—not because God puts it on you to punish you but because you move yourself out from under the protective covering of the blood of Jesus.

You must not let the devil dupe you into thinking you can live a disobedient lifestyle without consequences. The Bible clearly labels such thinking as a deception:

> *Be not deceived;* **God is not mocked: for whatsoever a man soweth, that shall he also reap.** *For he that soweth to his flesh shall of the flesh reap corruption;* **but he that soweth to the Spirit shall of the Spirit reap life everlasting.**
>
> —GALATIANS 6:7,8

Disobedience, or sin, interrupts your fellowship with God and separates you from His power. And as we saw in a previous chapter, a guilty conscience robs you of the confidence you need in order to receive from Him:

> **Beloved, if our heart condemn us not, then have we confidence toward God. And whatsoever we ask, we receive of him, because we keep his commandments, and do those things that are pleasing in his sight.**
>
> —1 JOHN 3:21,22

Some of the most dramatic healings I have ever seen during my years in the ministry have occurred when people simply got right with God. More often than not, the area of disobedience involved was related to anger, bitterness, resentment or unforgiveness.

For some spiritual reason, sins of unforgiveness frequently produce sickness or pain in a person's body. But any lifestyle choice that violates God's Word opens you to being oppressed by the devil in this way.

Unbelief

The third area of deception that contributes to sickness is unbelief. Unbelief is different from not knowing if it is the will of God to heal you, because the latter is rooted in ignorance. With the deception of unbelief, however, a person *knows* what the Word of God says on the matter yet still allows unbelief in his life.

The evidence of unbelief is fear. Faith promotes rest. Unbelief promotes fear.

As you saw in an earlier chapter, fear is having a greater belief in the devil's ability to bring harm to you than in God's ability to bring blessing.

Examine your heart for a moment. Is there a doctor's report you're fearful about? Is there a symptom in your body you're fearful about? If there is, you cannot allow that fear to remain. It is not all right to be afraid! If you are in fear, then you are not in faith, and you are opening a door to sickness and disease.

This may sound overly simplistic, but you deal with unbelief by doing what it takes to move over into a place of faith. Faith comes by repeatedly hearing the Word of God. (Rom. 10:17.)

You will know you are in faith when the fear is gone. **Fear hath torment** (1 John 4:18). Faith is peace and rest.

The Need To Fight

Make no mistake about it, coming to a place of faith concerning any of the promises of God requires some diligent effort. First Timothy 6:12 tells us that we must fight the good fight of faith in order to lay hold of eternal life.

Nevertheless, I frequently see people who face life-threatening conditions in their bodies who come to church only once a week—and yet spend four hours a night in front of the television set.

Sure, they do a few things that build faith, but overall their actions reveal that they are not taking the situation seriously.

To be honest, I sometimes want to grab them and shake them awake. I want to say, "What is the matter with you? Don't you realize that you are in a fight for your life? Satan doesn't take a break. He doesn't take the evening off to watch TV. If you are going to beat this thing, you will have to fight!"

Somebody who doesn't fight for his healing by using every available resource and every available moment in his day is deceived. I will say this without qualification. I have never seen anybody win a major battle with sickness and disease who didn't fight for it.

On the other hand, I have had the privilege of seeing numerous glorious testimonies of miraculous healings— many in the church I pastor—of people who were willing to fight the good fight of faith.

How do you do that? How do you fight for faith to receive your healing? First of all, you recognize that faith comes by hearing the Word of God. So you will have to fight to hear as much of God's Word about healing as you can. And you'll have to separate yourself from people who unwittingly try to speak death to you and instead fellowship with like-minded believers who will reinforce what you believe.

Fighting the good fight of faith means reading healing Scriptures and books about healing, listening to healing tapes and avoiding anyone or anything that speaks contrary to God's Word.

Satan will try to fill your mind with fear-filled thoughts of never being healed and of dying prematurely. You must fight to bring every thought captive to the obedience of Christ—particularly those that would exalt themselves above what you see in the Word regarding your healing:

> **Casting down imaginations, and every high thing that exalteth itself against the knowledge of God, and bringing into captivity every thought to the obedience of Christ.**
>
> —2 CORINTHIANS 10:5

My friend, you must fight to think only in line with God's Word. And you must fight to speak the right words. Life and death are in the power of the tongue. (Prov. 18:21.) Sadly, all too often people confronted with sickness just do not have the fight in them. They begin reasoning contrary to the truth, as we saw in James 1:22 (AMP). They might say something like, "Well, maybe it is my time to go home and be with the Lord." They begin questioning the will of God.

It is always easier to give up than to fight, but God does not condone quitting. Here is the question you need to ask yourself: *Do I want the healing that Jesus suffered to provide for me or not?* If you do, then you'll have to fight for it.

Now, it's interesting to note that throughout Paul's writings we find him using metaphors from boxing, wrestling and military warfare. There is a reason for that; he knew what many Christians are too deceived to realize— that if you are going to receive the healing Jesus purchased for you at Calvary, you had better be prepared to fight for it.

Magnifying Your Need

If Satan can't deceive you into quitting without a fight, he might try to push you into the other "ditch"—getting you to focus so totally on your need that you cease to be available to God to meet anybody else's.

As we've said before, this is exactly what locked Job into his negative situation. For forty-some chapters, he cried and moaned and groaned, "Why me, Lord?" But when Job finally took his eyes off his own problems and prayed for his friends, his deliverance came.

Often God's opening to meet your need comes as you make yourself available to Him to meet somebody else's. That's why Satan wants you to turn all of your attention inward. He will have you thinking that nobody is facing a greater challenge than you.

As we discussed, you need to fight for your healing, but don't make that the sole focus of all your efforts. Keep pressing toward the mark for the prize of the high calling of God in Christ Jesus. Get your eyes off yourself. Go pray and minister to somebody else. Speak to that infirmity and tell it that it is not going to stop you from witnessing, serving in the church or attending your prayer group.

Whatever you do, don't fall for the deception that causes you to be self-centered and self-absorbed.

The Need for Joy

Often, right before people lose a battle with sickness and disease, they seem to lose their joy. I have seen it happen repeatedly.

The statement **The joy of the Lord is your strength** (Neh. 8:10) is more than a Christian cliché; it's a biblical truth. The Word also says, **A merry heart doeth good like a medicine** (Prov. 17:22).

In the midst of your greatest challenges, it is vitally important that you cultivate joy.

In the first chapter of James, we find out why this is the case:

My brethren, count it all joy when ye fall into divers temptations [or tests and trials]; **knowing this, that the trying of your faith worketh patience. But let patience have her perfect work, that ye may be perfect and entire, wanting nothing.**

—JAMES 1:2,3

This isn't saying you are to be joyous *about* the temptation, test or trial. You are to rejoice, knowing that the trying of your faith works patience and that patience, having her perfect work, will result in your being perfect and entire, lacking nothing. The joy of the Lord is your source of spiritual strength to stand through a time of testing and trial.

The only way to stay joyous during a time of testing—especially during a severe attack of sickness or disease—is to know that if you don't quit, you win. You will come out on the other side of your trial being perfect and entire, wanting nothing. In the midst of your darkest night, you focus not on the challenge at hand but on the promise of what will happen in the end.

Every time you rejoice over that certainty, you get stronger. Every time you laugh at circumstances, the anointing goes up a notch. You absolutely must protect and increase your joy.

Allow me to remind you again not to allow yourself to be deceived into thinking it is not God's will to heal. Don't be deceived into thinking that you can live any way you want to. Don't be deceived into thinking you have to deal with fear in your life. Don't be deceived into thinking you don't need to fight with considerable diligence. Don't be deceived into thinking that nobody has a bigger problem than you and that it is all right to turn all of your attention inward.

And lastly, don't be deceived into thinking that you don't need to cultivate joy, for it is the spiritual strength you need to stand through a time of trial.

CHAPTER 12

Prayer will make a man cease from sin, or sin will entice a man to cease from prayer.

—John Bunyan[1]

Prayerlessness

I have saved the doorway to deception that I call "prayerlessness" until last because of the enormous power of the particular principle I am about to show you. If you don't apply this principle in your life, it truly is an open door to deception. If you do apply it though, it has the power to effectively close all the other doors we have already examined.

Let's look in Luke 22 at the final doorway to deception. There we have the account of Jesus and His disciples in the garden of Gethsemene. There is something significant I want you to see in verse 40:

> **When he was at the place, he said unto them, Pray that ye enter not into temptation.**

Jesus repeats this warning in verse 46:

> **Why sleep ye? rise and pray, lest ye enter into temptation.**

Twice Jesus warns His disciples that a failure to pray could lead to temptation. Satan, of course, is the tempter. Remember, James 1:13 says: **Let no man say when he is**

tempted, I am tempted [tested or tried] **of God: for God cannot be tempted with evil, neither tempteth he any man.**

Satan cannot draw you into temptation unless he can deceive you. He can't force you into temptation. He has to deceive you into *choosing* to enter in by your own free will.

Since you won't fall prey to temptation without deception, I believe we can safely and accurately insert the word *deception* into Luke 22:46, thus rendering it: "Rise and pray, lest you enter into *deception.*"

The principle being presented here is this: Prayer has the power to close the door on every form of deception Satan tries to promote in your life.

When Jesus walked this earth, He revealed the truth. He preached the Word to multitudes, and on many occasions He further explained it to His inner circle.

After His ascension Jesus sent the Holy Spirit in His place to do the very same thing for us.

The Holy Spirit is called the Spirit of Truth (John 16:13), and as Jesus said, **He shall teach you all things, and bring to your remembrance, whatsoever I have said unto you** (John 14:26).

If you are lacking truth in some area or don't understand a certain passage of Scripture, the Holy Spirit's ministry is to bring the Word of God to your remembrance or reveal the meaning of Scriptures you don't understand.

Prayer is the way you access this ministry. It is the way you receive revelation of the truth—truth by which you recognize deception and choose not to enter into it.

In fact, this is the way you can close the door to all deception in your life. Satan will see to it that tests, trials and temptations come, but the proper application of the power of prayer in your life will keep you from being deceived.

Speak the Wisdom of God in a Mystery

Exactly how do you pray for this revelation knowledge? We find part of the answer to that question in 1 Corinthians 2:7-8:

> ***We speak the wisdom of God in a mystery,*** **even the hidden wisdom, which God ordained before the world unto our glory: which none of the princes of this world knew: for had they known it, they would not have crucified the Lord of glory.**

The word *mystery* here means something that is initially hidden from your natural or intellectual understanding.

Verse 9 goes on to refer to another hidden thing—the will of God for your life:

> **As it is written, Eye hath not seen, nor ear heard, neither have entered into the heart of man, the things which God hath prepared for them that love him.**

There are a lot of things about God's plan for your life that He keeps a mystery for the same reason He kept Christ's resurrection a mystery: If Satan and his crowd knew all of God's plans for you, they would know where to concentrate their efforts in trying to stop it from unfolding.

However, verses 10 and 12 tell us one way in which God can show us these things:

> **God hath revealed them unto us by his Spirit....
> Now we have received, not the spirit of the world,
> but the spirit which is of God; [Why?] that we might
> know the things that are freely given to us of God.**

Here you can plainly see that the Holy Spirit has been given
to you to reveal the things God has for you. These are the things
that await you in God's plan for your life here on earth.

Verse 13 goes on to tell us how the Holy Spirit does this:

> **Which things also we speak, not in the words which
> man's wisdom teacheth, but which the Holy Ghost
> teacheth; comparing spiritual things with spiritual.**

As usual, *The Amplified Bible* enhances our understanding. In it, verse 13 reads,

> **We are setting these truths forth in words not taught
> by human wisdom but taught by the [Holy] Spirit,
> combining and interpreting spiritual truths with spir-
> itual language *[to those who possess the Holy Spirit]*.**

Notice that it doesn't say "to those who are born again."
Paul wrote this letter to a company of born-again believers,
so there would be no point in adding **to those who possess
the Holy Spirit** unless there were some who didn't.

But his adding that phrase seems indicates that being
born again isn't enough in order to understand some spiritual truths; you must possess the Holy Spirit.

The key to understanding this point is in the word *possess*.
The literal meaning of the Greek word from which it is
translated means "embracing in all its fullness."[2]

When you are born again you become a temple of the Holy Spirit, but you are not automatically filled with the Holy Spirit the moment you become a temple. That is the role of the baptism in the Holy Spirit. It results in a complete "embracing" of all the fullness of the Spirit.

There Is More

If you are one of the many Christians who have been taught that you receive all of the Holy Spirit you are ever going to get the moment you are born again, please keep your heart open as I show you a couple of Scriptures from the book of Acts.

In Acts 19:2, Paul approaches a group of new Christians in Ephesus and asks them an interesting question:

Have ye received the Holy Ghost since ye believed?

What's their answer? Look at verse 3.

We have not so much as heard whether there be any Holy Ghost.

And a few verses later we read:

And when Paul had laid his hands upon them, the Holy Ghost came on them; and they spake with tongues, and prophesied.

—ACTS 19:6

Acts chapter 8 also demonstrates quite clearly that there is more of the Holy Spirit available to you after you are born again.

Then Philip went down to the city of Samaria, and preached Christ unto them.... When they believed Philip preaching the things concerning the kingdom

of God, and the name of Jesus Christ, they were baptized [born again].... Now when the apostles which were at Jerusalem heard that Samaria had received the word of God, they sent unto them Peter and John: who, when they were come down, prayed for them, that they might receive the Holy Ghost: (for as yet he was fallen upon none of them: only they were baptized [born again] in the name of the Lord Jesus.) Then laid they their hands on them, and they received the Holy Ghost.

—ACTS 8:5,12,14-17

Either directly or indirectly, every scriptural mention of the baptism in the Holy Spirit accompanies a reference to speaking in other tongues. Tongues are clearly the evidence that proves you have received the baptism in the Holy Spirit.

Furthermore, the Bible says that Jesus is the One who baptizes in the Holy Ghost and fire and that He is the same yesterday, today and forever. (Matt. 3:11; Heb. 13:8.) That means if Jesus baptized in the Holy Spirit yesterday, then He is still doing it today and He will be doing it tomorrow.

Pray That You May Interpret

Here is what I want to make sure you see from all of these Scriptures we have examined. The key to avoiding deception is walking in revealed truth—and the level of revealed truth you walk in is a function of having the fullness of the Holy Spirit's operating in your life. His ministry is to reveal to you the things God has prepared for you. You can't know them without Him because they are a mystery to your natural mind.

First Corinthians 14:2 confirms what I am telling you:

For he that speaketh in an unknown tongue speaketh not unto men, but unto God: for no man understandeth him; howbeit in the spirit *he speaketh mysteries.*

According to the Bible, when you pray in tongues you speak mysteries to God that are hidden from your natural understanding. One of those mysteries is God's plan and purpose for your life. When you pray in tongues, you may very well be talking to God about the things He has prepared for you. In the Spirit you can unravel that mystery and gain understanding of those things.

"But, Pastor Mac, you said it is the Holy Spirit's job to reveal God's plan to me. How can I know the plan if I can't understand what I am speaking?"

First Corinthians 14:13 holds your answer:

Wherefore let him that speaketh in an unknown tongue pray that he may interpret.

Your understanding doesn't have to be unfruitful. God is not trying to keep His will a secret from *you* but from the forces of darkness that would otherwise pose obstacles to that plan. God *wants* to reveal His plan to you. If you will just ask for the interpretation when you pray in tongues, He can reveal it to you without revealing it to the enemy.

Now, if all this sounds more than just a little strange to you, 1 Corinthians 2:14 tells why you might not be able to make much sense of it:

But the natural man receiveth not the things of the Spirit of God: for they are foolishness unto him: neither can he know them, because they are spiritually discerned.

The only way these things will make any sense to you is for the Spirit of God to reveal them to you. For that to occur, the Bible says you need to be one of those who possess the baptism of the Holy Spirit in all its fullness. Then as you pray in tongues believing you will interpret, things will become clear to you. The Spirit will give you a revelation of truth in your life, and that is your greatest defense against deception.

Mysteries You Need To Know

God's plan for your life won't be the only mystery you will be in the dark about if you don't have the ministry of the Holy Spirit operating in your life. Allow me to show you some of the other mysteries God wants to reveal to you by His Spirit.

In Mark chapter 4 we find the parable of the sower. This is a case in which even Jesus' disciples didn't understand what He was saying. Verses 10 and 11 make this evident:

When he [Jesus] was alone, they that were about him with the twelve asked of him the parable. And he said unto them, Unto you it is given to know the mystery of the kingdom of God: but unto them that are without, all these things are done in parables.

In other words, Jesus is telling His disciples that they are *supposed* to understand the mystery He is revealing to them.

This is in contrast to others who heard Jesus, as He explains in verse 12:

> **That seeing they may see, and not perceive; and hearing they may hear, and not understand; lest at any time they should be converted, and their sins should be forgiven them.**

You see, the unsaved don't have the capacity to understand the Word of God. But once they are converted, they have access to the mysteries of the Word.

What is important for you to see here is that even though it was given to the disciples to understand the parable, they didn't get it. They had to ask Jesus to explain it to them, which He did.

Now, Jesus isn't on this earth to explain His Word anymore, but He did send the Spirit of Truth to do that for us in His place. Just as the disciples had questions, there will be times when you, too, will have questions about something you read in the Word.

At those times, all you need to do is sit quietly and begin praying in the Holy Spirit, believing for the interpretation and expecting understanding to come. The revelation *will* come. The mystery will begin to unfold because it is given to you to understand the mysteries of God's Word.

Christ in You

Let's look at another mystery, one we see in Colossians 1:26-27:

> **Even the mystery which hath been hid from the ages and from generations, but now is made manifest**

to his saints: to whom God would make known what is the riches of the glory of this mystery among the Gentiles; which is Christ in you, the hope of glory.

Friend, once you have a revelation of who lives inside you—when you realize that the Greater One indwells you— there will never be a "Goliath," never be a mountain and never be a circumstance that will make you bow in fear. You will charge every Goliath, you will cast every mountain into the sea and you will overcome every circumstance when you *know* Christ is in you.

This revelation will make you a world changer. But unless the mystery of Christ in you is real to you, the quality of your life will be indistinguishable from that of someone who is unsaved.

Ask God to reveal this mystery to your heart as you pray in tongues. You will begin to know that you are more than a conqueror and you can do all things through Christ. You will become a winner just looking for a race to run.

The Mystery of Marriage

The Bible mentions another mystery in Ephesians 5:30-32:

For we are members of his body, of his flesh, and of his bones. For this cause shall a man leave his father and mother, and shall be joined unto his wife, and they two shall be one flesh. *This is a great mystery:* but I speak concerning Christ and the church.

There are actually two parts to this mystery.

The first concerns the mystery of how to have a successful marriage: It will forever be a mystery to you until you and your partner begin praying in the Holy Ghost together.

When you do, the Spirit of God begins to reveal to you the sacredness of your relationship. God strengthens your marriage and transforms it into what He meant it to be. Suddenly, you are simply unable to stay mad at each other anymore. And nothing is able to divide you from one another.

When you spend time praying in the Spirit together, the Holy Spirit also shows you how to treat your spouse. He gives you encouraging words to give your mate. He shows you special gifts to buy or tells you when to do something special for your beloved. Day by day, He teaches you how to get along with and truly love your husband or wife.

Praying in the Spirit together absolutely revolutionizes your marriage.

The second part of this mystery deals with your relationship to the Body of Christ—your place in the local church to which God has called you.

As I've mentioned before, God has a place for you in the Body of Christ. It is a place where you can bring your unique supply of natural and spiritual gifts, which enable your church to grow and be successful in expanding God's kingdom.

In return, it is also a place where you can receive the teaching, anointing and spiritual gifts—the life flow from God—that you need to grow into the person God wants you to be.

Unfortunately, many Christians are not connected to a local part of the Body of Christ—or they are connected to the wrong part—because they don't understand this mystery. You must be connected to a local church. And the Holy Spirit will reveal which one is right for you and what place you best fit within it.

In the Twinkling of an Eye

There is yet another mystery the Spirit wants to reveal to you. You can find this one in 1 Corinthians 15:51. In fact, your understanding of this mystery will have a profound effect on your Christian walk:

> **Behold, I shew you a *mystery;* we shall not all sleep, but we shall all be changed, in a moment, in the twinkling of an eye, at the last trump: for the trumpet shall sound, and the dead shall be raised incorruptible, and we shall be changed.**

This is the Rapture, or the catching away of the Church, but the Bible calls it a mystery. That is why so many Christians have never been able to embrace this truth as reality. Yet this is one of the most important revelations you can have where your daily walk with God is concerned.

Let me explain. Do you ever have trouble with your flesh? Has your old man not entirely passed away? (Rom. 6:6; Eph. 4:22.) If so, the revelation of this mystery to your heart will help set you on a straight and narrow path.

When the fact that Jesus could return right now is as real to you as the chair on which you are sitting, when the fact that Heaven could be just a breath away becomes that real to you, you won't take a chance of getting caught in some willful sin.

When the Rapture of the Church is a reality to you, you will begin to be separate and sanctify yourself to God's holy purpose. As it says in 1 John 3:2-3:

> **Beloved, now are we the sons of God, and it doth not yet appear what we shall be: but we know that, when he shall appear, we shall be like him; for we shall see him as he is. And every man that hath this hope in him purifieth himself, even as he is pure.**

Now, the Spirit of God can reveal this mystery to your spirit in prayer. And once He does, you will never be the same.

Praying in the Spirit

My friend, you can radically change your life by letting the Holy Spirit conduct His ministry of revelation to your heart. Prayer with your natural understanding is important, but it is just not enough. You don't have the intellectual discernment to know how and what to pray precisely, because so many of the significant things in life are *mysteries*.

Romans 8:26-27 (NAS) says it this way:

> **And in the same way the Spirit also helps our weakness; for we do not know how to pray as we should, but the Spirit Himself intercedes for us with groanings too deep for words; and He who searches the hearts knows what the mind of the Spirit is, because He intercedes for the saints according to the will of God.**

The *New English Bible* renders the last part of verse 26 this way:

But through our inarticulate groans the Spirit himself is pleading for us.

Please don't allow yourself to be cheated out of your heavenly prayer language. You need to be *baptized* in the Holy Spirit once definitively and then *filled* with the Spirit on a continual basis. (Eph. 5:18.)

The more of the Spirit that operates in your life, the more consistently revelation knowledge will flow. And the more you understand truth, the more you will be able to avoid deception, thereby withstanding the temptations, tests and trials that Satan lays for you.

Closing the Door to Deception

Deception is the opposite of truth. Ultimately, prayerlessness is a major doorway to deception because it keeps you from receiving revelation knowledge of the truth.

The primary reason for prayerlessness is not knowing *how* to pray. It is just that simple.

The solution is to be baptized in the Holy Spirit with the evidence of speaking in other tongues and then regularly yielding yourself to His ministry in your devotional time by praying in tongues. That's how you avoid the snares, traps, pitfalls and deceptions that Satan sets for you.

You will know the truth, and the truth will set and keep you free because **if Satan can't deceive you, he can't defeat you!**

Endnotes

Chapter 1
[1] Strong, "Greek," entry #3180, p. 47.

Chapter 2
[1] Sweeting, p. 155.
[2] Barna, p. 117.
[3] Ibid
[4] Sweeting, p. 447.
[5] Lawrence and Lanbach, p. 44.

Chapter 3
[1] Sweeting, p. 19.
[2] Strong, "Greek," entry #s 202, 189, p. 9.
[3] Strong, "Greek," entry #s 1950, 1953, p. 31.

Chapter 4
[1] Sweeting, p. 455.
[2] Vine, s.v. "love," Vol. 3, pp. 20-22.
[3] Strong, "Greek," entry #2889, p. 43.

Chapter 5
[1] Sweeting, p. 38.

Chapter 6
[1] Sweeting, p. 105.

Chapter 7
[1] Strong, "Greek," entry #4166, p. 59.

Chapter 8
[1] Sweeting, p. 369.
[2] Mead, p. 357.

Chapter 9
[1] Sweeting, p. 369.
[2] Strong, "Greek," entry #2222, p. 35.

Chapter 10
[1] Mead, p. 383.
[2] Vine, s.v. "love," Vol. 3, pp. 20-22.
[3] Vine, s.v. "rich," Vol. 3, pp. 295-296.

Chapter 12
[1] Sweeting, p. 362.
[2] Vine, s.v. "possess," Vol. 3, pp. 193-194.

References

Barna, George. *Virtual America: What Every Christian Needs to Know About Ministering in an Age of Spiritual, Cultural and Technological Revolution.* Ventura: Regal Books, 1994.

Lawrence, Brother and Frank C. Lanbach. *Practicing His Presence.* Massachusetts: Paraclete Press, 1985.

Mead, Frank S. *12,000 Religious Quotations.* Grand Rapids: Baker Book House, 1989.

Strong, James. *Strong's Exhaustive Concordance of the Bible.* "Hebrew and Chaldee Dictionary," "Greek Dictionary of the New Testament." Nashville: Abingdon, 1890.

Sweeting, George. *Who Said That?* Chicago: Moody Press, 1994.

Vine, W. E. *Expository Dictionary of New Testament Words.* Old Tappan: Fleming H. Revell, 1940.

About the Author

Mac Hammond is the founder and senior pastor of Living Word Christian Center, a large and growing church in Minneapolis, Minnesota. Pastor Hammond also hosts a weekly, one-hour television broadcast called *The Winner's Way, With Mac Hammond,* which is seen nationwide, and a daily sixty-second television commentary called *The Winner's Minute.*

Hammond has authored several internationally distributed books and is broadly acclaimed for his ability to apply the principles of the Bible to practical situations and the challenges of daily living.

To contact Mac Hammond,
write:

Mac Hammond

P. O. Box 29469

Minneapolis, Minnesota 55429

Please include your prayer requests
and comments when you write.

Other Books by Mac Hammond

Seeing and Knowing

Angels at Your Service

The Last Millinnium

Additional copies of this book
are available from your local bookstore.

HARRISON HOUSE
Tulsa, Oklahoma 74153

The Harrison House Vision

Proclaiming the truth and the power
Of the Gospel of Jesus Christ
With excellence;

Challenging Christians to
Live victoriously,
Grow spiritually,
Know God intimately.